NO PLANE CRASHES ON 9/11
Exposing The Illusion

Essays by

Kevin Barrett
Ronald Bleier
Elias Davidsson
Carl Lesnor
Nicholas Lysson

Edited by
Ronald Bleier

Acknowledgments

"Pre- And Post-9/11 False Flags: How Weapons of Mass Deception Are Interdependent" first appeared in *We Are NOT Charlie Hebdo!: Free Thinkers Question the French 9/11*. Copyright © 2015 Kevin Barrett. Reprinted by permission of the author.

"Introduction", "WTC Building 7, the Smoking Gun?", "9/11, An Inside Job? A Review Essay Based on David Ray Griffin's Research", "Webster Tarpley and Rogue Networks", ""No Planes on 9/11 – Exposing the Illusion", "No Planes on 911 - The Two Minute Video", "Did Cheney Plan to Assassinate President Bush on 9/11?" first appeared on Desip.igc.org. Copyright © 2005-2019 Ronald Bleier. Reprinted by permission of the author.

"Excerpts from 9/11, The Betrayal of America" first appeared in *The Betrayal of America*. Copyright © 2018 Elias Davidsson. Reprinted by permission of the author.

"Robert Fisk on 9/11 Truth: Good Beginning, Bob" first appeared on Desip.igc.org. Copyright © 2007 Carl Lesnor. Reprinted by permission of the author.

"9/11: Revelations and Reflections" first appeared on Desip.igc.org. Copyright © 2007 Nicholas Lysson. Reprinted by permission of the author.

Table of Contents

David Ray Griffin

Gerard Holmgren

INTRODUCTION

By Ronald Bleier

June 2019

T

he bulk of this volume is taken up with the five articles on 9/11 I've written from 2005 to 2015 (plus two in 2019), pushing back against the official account that the terror attacks of that day were to be blamed on Al Qaeda, led by Osama bin Laden. The remaining articles by four other contributors – Carl Lesnor, Nicholas Lysson and selections from books by Elias Davisson and Kevin Barrett -- all support my understanding that 9/11 was an inside job, a false flag operation directed by the highest levels of the United States government, intending the launch of a Global War on Terror (GWOT), the pretext for permanent war.

My first three articles were inspired largely by the work of David Ray Griffin, author of about fifteen books exposing much of the reality behind the 9/11 terror events. A retired professor of religion at the Claremont School of Theology, Claremont, California, Dr. Griffin is widely acclaimed for the depth of his research, his mastery of detail and the clarity and economy of his exposition. I sought out Dr. Griffin's work after I saw a one-hour documentary in 2003 that convinced me that controlled demolition was the only way steel-framed, high-rise buildings could have been brought down at virtually the speed of gravity in their own footprint. In that case, then Osama bin Laden (OBL) could not have been responsible.

While I'm still a great fan of the work of Dr. Griffin, we split paths after I read a ten-page article entitled "Manufactured Terrorism: The Truth About 9/11," by the late Gerard Holmgren, an Australian researcher, (d. 2010, age 51).

Holmgren's article convinced me that there were no airline plane crashes that day. My two articles on the theory of No Planes on 9/11 in 2006 and 2015 summarize the evidence and the arguments that Holmgren, Morgan Reynolds, and others, have brought to light in support of the No Planes Theory. (NPT)

Except for certain sections of my first article based on Dr. Griffin's first two 9/11 books[1] all of the articles in this volume present evidence consistent with the NPT. Two of the contributors, the late Carl Lesnor and the evergreen Nicholas Lysson, do not directly take up the NPT, but my selection from Elias Davidsson's as yet unpublished book, *The Betrayal of America: Revisiting the 9/11 Evidence,* supports no planes by pointing to the lack of plane wreckage; the absence of credible evidence that hijackings took place, or evidence that Arabs boarded planes on Sept 11.

Contributing author Kevin Barrett also rejects the meme of Arab hijackers, and passenger plane hijackings on 9/11 even while he is agnostic on the theory of no planes. In an April 2019 email to me he wrote:

> The official story of the allegedly hijacked planes is obviously false—there were no Arabs on the planes and no hijackings (with the possible exception of remote hijackings)—but how the illusion of "crashed hijacked planes" was created is a mystery that requires further investigation, preferably in the context of prosecutions.

The importance of determining whether or not there were hijackings, or whether passenger planes crashed into buildings on 9/11 cannot be overstated. As Morgan Reynolds points out, the "key to acquiescence in the government's war on terror and global domination project is public belief in Arab hi-jacked airliners and crashes."

Piloting a Passenger Jet into a High Rise is Practically Impossible

Only years after 9/11 did I learn that the videos repeatedly shown on TV of a plane crashing into the World Trade Center's South Tower were computer-generated images (CGI). I also learned that to pilot a large passenger jet into a high rise is so difficult to achieve as to be practically impossible. For example, a jet airliner, flying at speeds of 500-600 mph would face uncontrollable turbulence at sea level due to relatively dense atmospheric pressures.[2]

Moreover, I learned that even the most experienced pilots would be unable to successfully strike a high-rise target without extensive practice on a simulator. It's doubtful that any of the nominal Arab pilots, none of whom it was claimed trained on a jet plane, and one of whom reportedly couldn't even get a beginner's pilot's license, would have access to such simulators even if they existed.[3]

Anecdotal Objections to the NPT

1. Eyewitness Testimony

Once I became an NPT adherent, I found that I typically faced two major objections. Eyewitness testimony was the most common challenge: people typically cited friends or family who swear they saw a plane striking the WTC Tower. While adherents to the official narrative may not find it convincing that research has demonstrated that eyewitness testimony is unreliable, they don't address the other side of this question. For example, Gerard Holmgren has pointed to eyewitnesses who testified to seeing a small plane or missile rather than an airliner crashing into the Towers. Holmgren also found there was eyewitness testimony that there was no plane at all.

Memory contamination of eyewitness testimony on 9/11 is also likely to be a significant factor since the official narrative of hijacked passenger planes was strongly implanted in the public mind, not least, by strategically placed "expert" spokespeople who supported the plane fakery and who pointed to Al-Qaeda, and OBL and Arab hijackers as the responsible parties within hours or less of the attacks.[4] In addition, there is evidence that there was a dummy airplane flyover at the site of the Pentagon crash and there may well have been such a dummy plane in NYC as well.[5]

There are also competing eyewitness testimonies of timely explosions on several levels of the towers, including the basement and sub-basement levels, which many 9/11 truthers think are signs that controlled demolition brought down the Twin Towers.

There are evidently fewer eyewitness claims of the strike on the North Tower simply because there was no reason before 8:46 a.m. that day to expect such an event. Also, the widely viewed video of the first strike, the so-called Naudet tape, reveals that what struck the North Tower was not an airline passenger plane -- Gerard Holmgren calls it a "whatsit" -- moves so rapidly – in only one second, from 1.10 to 1.11 minutes on the video -- that fewer witnesses came forward to claim that they saw it in real-time.[6]

2. What Happened to the Airline Passengers?

If there were no plane crashes on 9/11 then what happened to the 266 airline passengers that the government claims lost their lives that day? (It turns out the real number of airline victims may be as few as 66.) For many years, I had no answer to this pertinent question, though I was clear that they somehow, somewhere, must have been murdered by U.S. authorities since I didn't believe they died in plane crashes.

It wasn't until years later that I understood more about the cell phone calls purportedly made on 9/11 from cruising airliners that a credible scenario emerged. I finally learned that cell phone calls could not be made from 40,000 feet since jet planes fly too quickly for the electronic "handshake" to be made – the transfer of location and identification signals from one cell phone tower on the ground to the next. If the cell phone calls were not made from the air, then the 9/11 calls must have been made from the ground, as subsequent research demonstrates. A large section of Elias Davidsson's book on *Hijacking America's Mind: Counterfeiting the 9/11 Evidence* (2013), analyzes the details of the 9/11 phone calls, and points to anomalies in every call, indicating they could not have been made from the air.

Davidsson also points to the circumstantial evidence of the absence of airplane background noise, such as the hum of the engines that we would normally expect. Missing also is the commotion connected to hijacking incidents, which, in these cases, purportedly included the grisly murder of pilots and co-pilots. Instead, the 9/11 calls are made by typically unflustered passengers, and in one case by a calm stewardess. Callers soberly described nearby scenes of stabbing and other mayhem.

Evidence corroborating ground-to-ground cell phone calls appears in the section on the cell phone calls in Massimo Mazzucco's in-depth 5-hour documentary available on YouTube, "September 11 - The New Pearl Harbor." In one exemplary case, Mazzucco replays the brief call of Cee Cee Lyles, a flight attendant on United 93 who managed, in her last words, to whisper to her husband, "it's a frame."[7] Evidently, she had been told to say that she was witnessing a hijacking. Most poignantly, in her brief call, she was also able to hint that she understood that she didn't expect to see her husband and children again.

More important detail comes from a retired flight attendant and author, Rebekah Roth, in her series of novels based on what she believes really happened on 9/11 (*Methodical Illusion* (2015), *Methodical Deception* (2015) *Methodical Conclusion* (2016), etc.).

Roth outlined a credible scenario of how the ill-fated passengers and crew were rounded up and flown to a secluded airfield in upstate New York. As per Roth's scenario, after they landed, most of the passengers and crew were gassed to death while they waited on the tarmac. Meanwhile, some of the victims had been deplaned and were persuaded to make scripted cell phone calls, on the pretext that they were taking part in a national security drill before they too must have been dispatched.

The Prospects

It has become distressingly clear that the world of George Orwell's *1984* mirrors our political situation today. Those in control of ruthless criminal governments have learned the lesson that no matter how transparent their outrages are, they can get away with murder and mass murder since they retain full control of the investigative agencies and co-opt significant portions of the media.

The reason we can, with maximum confidence, point to both the JFK assassination and the 9/11 terror attacks as inside jobs is because of the efforts of many hundreds of researchers who have risen to these high-profile challenges. The information they have collectively uncovered has, to a significant degree, enabled us to pull aside the curtain of confusion.

Nevertheless, the prospects for national consensus on 9/11 truth are, to say the least, not good. As we near the end of the second decade of the 21st century, the official narrative of an al-Qaeda terror plot on 9/11, justifying global war as national policy seems settled on an unshakable foundation.

There appears no better prospect for unmasking such perpetrators as George W. Bush, Dick Cheney, Donald Rumsfeld, George Tenet, Rudy Giuliani et.al, than there so far has been for unmasking LBJ and Allen Dulles, as the masterminds of the JFK assassination. Indeed, the two attacks are indissolubly linked.

Without the former, we can reasonably speculate that there would have been no opportunity for the latter, and the world would not be in its present straits.

Nevertheless, while we live and breathe, we do what we can to spread the word.
Without hope, there is no hope. □

***

ROBERT FISK ON 9/11 TRUTH: GOOD BEGINNING, BOB

By Carl Lesnor

September 2007

*The government's failure to provide an open
investigation of this disaster is the real scandal; one
colluded in by the American political oligarchy and the
media that serves it.*

--CARL LESNOR

Editor's Notes

I give this article by my late friend, Carl Lesnor, pride of place because his lucid, incisive (not-to-say enviable), prose makes for bracing reading as well as it aptly serves to begin the discussion. Among much else, Carl reminds us of that brief period, ending perhaps in 2007 or 2008 when left spokespeople like Robert Fisk, Alexander Cockburn, Tariq Ali, and others, contended with 9/11 truth activists - -Fisk calls them "ravers" (as in stark, raving, mad). For this period, ravers persisted in expressing their unhappiness with the refusal or the inability of these luminaries to address the glaring evidence that 9/11 was an inside job.

...

Robert Fisk has written an article in the *Independent* entitled "Even I question the Truth About 9/11" (2007) that has attracted a great deal of attention and a certain amount of controversy.[8] Fisk begins by complaining about the "ravers" as he calls them, who come to his lectures about the Middle East and accuse him of covering up the truth about the events of September 11. He usually replies that he is a Middle East correspondent and has no special knowledge of what happened to the World Trade Center, that he has "quite enough real plots on my hands in Lebanon, Iraq, Syria, Iran, the Gulf, etc., to worry about imaginary ones in Manhattan."

Still, he has questions. More questions than answers but raising questions about the government's account on the part of a famous and respected journalist is a notable event. He concludes his column by repeating that he is not a "conspiracy theorist" but that he'd like to know the full story, not least because it was the trigger for the disaster in Iraq, Afghanistan, and much of the Middle East.

He has been taken to task, sometimes gently, sometimes harshly, by people in the "truth movement" for being too ambiguous, for engaging in "doublethink" and by repeating in the last paragraph that he is not a "conspiracy theorist" (though he concludes by saying that he'd like to know more).

Much depends on the words "conspiracy theory" and how it used. Let's begin at the beginning. Some of us who are old enough, remember that this expression dates from the time of the JFK assassination when, in the face of overwhelming evidence that the bullets came from two directions, the Warren commission claimed that they were all fired from the rear by a lone assassin. Thus, the notorious "magic bullet" theory. Rejecting this theory automatically led to an inescapable conclusion: that if there were two or more assassins there was a conspiracy. That's how the law defines it. (Unless, of course, two lone assassins, unknown to one another opened fire at the same time.) If the magic bullet theory is true, the assassination can be explained in terms of psychology, but if it's false, then it becomes a political issue.

Naturally, the political implications of a conspiracy were enormous and inevitably led to speculation about the identities and motives of the conspirators. Much of the dispute was about these implications and people tended to take positions based on their political predispositions and to reason backwards. The trajectory of the bullets was determined not by ballistics, but by political beliefs and loyalties.

Those who trusted the government considered it disloyal to question its word. Those who considered Kennedy merely another servant of an omnipotent ruling class denied that its agents would have any interest in killing him. ([Noam Chomsky and Alexander Cockburn maintain this position to this day.)[9]

Those who were relieved that the "Marxist" assassin was not being accused of acting on behalf of the Soviets or the Cubans, which they feared might lead to war, (like I.F. Stone) preferred to let sleeping dogs lie and not question the inconsistencies in the official story. Fortified by their devotion to this noble end, they had no compunction in attacking those who challenged the authorized version.

Those who were counting on the Kennedy family to challenge the Commission report took their failure to do as a reason to endorse it, though Robert Kennedy --as well as family friend, Arthur Schlesinger -- were careful to say that they "accepted" it but hadn't actually read it. ([It has now been revealed that Robert Kennedy never believed it: see the review of Brothers: The Hidden History of the Kennedy Years by David Talbot.

All of these people used the term "conspiracy theory" to discredit those who questioned the official findings and had no trouble finding far-fetched theories as proof that all skeptics were the victims of paranoid delusions --- yet it is obvious that conspiracies have always existed and that no political history that rejects them A PRIORI is possible.

The events of September 11, 2001, present an entirely different question, for in this case the official version is itself a conspiracy theory and, on its face, quite an implausible one. To begin with there are the obvious questions of how such a vast operation could have succeeded in overcoming US defenses. If the government was completely taken by surprise by this conspiracy in the morning, unable even to mount a defense of the Pentagon hours after the first alert was received, how could it have known just who was behind it in the afternoon? The nature of the evidence it presented -- the incriminating documents left in the rental car and in the suitcase that never made it aboard the plane, the passport that came floating down at the crash site -- was enough to arouse suspicions. The accumulation of conflicting stories and implausible events in the following days only strengthened them. (For a list of seventy --but by no means all -- of the reasons to doubt the official story see: 70 reasons to doubt the official 9/11 story)

But implausible doesn't necessarily mean impossible and suspicions aren't always justified; more complete information can dispel them. But in this instance, the behavior of the government in refusing to provide such evidence, stonewalling appeals for investigations, lying, and destroying evidence could only increase them. As in the Kennedy assassination, the cover-up itself can be seen as part of the conspiracy and cannot fail to fuel suspicions that give rise to conflicting theories, theories that not only conflict with the official story, but inevitably with one another. Some of them might seem fanciful; some indeed are, but this cannot simply be ascribed to the "paranoia" of those who put them forward and used as an argument for accepting the government story. The government's failure to provide an open investigation of this disaster is the real scandal; one colluded in by the American political oligarchy and the media that serves it.

This doesn't mean that all who accepted, persuaded themselves to accept, or thought it prudent to accept the official story are equally culpable; many refused to listen to conflicting evidence for fear of its implications. Shortly after the attack on the twin towers, I attended a talk given at Columbia University by a noted British radical, Tariq Ali, who spoke about its political implications. During the question period, he was taken aback by the widespread disbelief in the official account on the part of his New York audience. When asked whether he actually believed it, he replied that he didn't want to think about it. In addition to this fear, which was shared by many, we might add the fear of ridicule, the fear of being discredited by being seen as embracing "irresponsible" speculation.

Refusal to open Pandora's box, disinclination to isolate oneself, to risk undermining one's political credibility for fear of being branded a "loony"--all this might not be admirable, but it is certainly understandable. Fisk's emerging doubts, however guarded and tentative, should be welcomed, for the question is not whether or not he is waffling, but finding out what happened. If we welcome his first step on the road to truth, we can ask him to be consistent and take the next step.[10]

Fisk gives the impression of trying to allay his increasing doubts by pulling the well-worn but comforting blanket of "incompetence" over his head.[11]

This is the last refuge of the denier of conspiracies, for it is undeniably true that government officials -- as much as, or more than others -- often produce disasters through mere incompetence and "stupidity." But this argument only goes so far: taken to its logical extreme, it can be used to deny any and all purposeful action. That there are unintended consequences doesn't mean that there are no intended ones. This becomes painfully obvious when Fisk writes:

"My final argument – a clincher, in my view – is that the Bush administration has screwed up everything – militarily, politically diplomatically – it has tried to do in the Middle East; so how on earth could it successfully bring off the international crimes against humanity in the United States on 11 September 2001?

"Well, I still hold to that view. Any military which can claim – as the Americans did two days ago – that al-Qaida is on the run is not capable of carrying out anything on the scale of 9/11."

The obvious objection to his last sentence is that the U.S. claim is not an error, but a lie. Surely Fisk understands that there's a difference between what a military spokesman claims and what he actually believes. After spending a lifetime listening to them, he cannot possibly believe them honest but dim-witted. Similarly, his assertion that the administration has screwed up everything it has tried to do in the Middle East rests on the assumption that the stated reasons for its intervention were the real reasons. (Or else that he has discerned what the 'real' reasons are, but that they, too, conflict with what Cheney-Bush have brought about.) The poor man is suffering; he would like to be able to get back to sleep, but the incompetent comforter isn't going to succeed in shutting out the light. He would like to believe it is "a clincher," but he already knows that it isn't. □

WTC BUILDING 7 – THE 911 SMOKING GUN?

by Ronald Bleier

March 2005

Editor's Notes

The first book I read that debunked the official account of 9/11 was Eric Hufschmid's *Painful Questions; An Analysis of the September 11th Attack* (2002), still a book well worth reading. Hufschmid was skeptical about hijackers, although at that early date he believed that planes actually crashed into the WTC. He speculates (incorrectly) that the planes must have been remotely controlled. This 2,000-word article is largely based on his research.

W

as 9/11 an inside job? Take 10 minutes to review video of the third building to collapse on 9/11, WTC Building 7; and a related slide show and then follow the logic:[12] If Building 7 was destroyed through a controlled demolition so were the Twin Towers. If the Twin Towers were destroyed by demolition than Osama Bin Laden and his alleged conspirators didn't do it.

One of the difficulties in determining whether or not to believe the official story about 9/11, is the enormous amount of information available on the Internet, in books, and perhaps a dozen videos dedicated to 9/11 inquiry. The very plethora of information (and disinformation) is daunting to many who can't afford the time and energy to sift through the torrent of data and analysis in a timely manner

One quick solution to help interested people decide whether 9/11 was an inside job is to recommend David Ray Griffin's *The New Pearl Harbor* (2004).[13] Griffin's book is a masterpiece of concise and coherent compilation of the available plausible evidence indicating that the official story -- that the attacks of 9/11 were planned and executed by al-Qaeda terrorists – cannot be accurate.

For those who are not yet ready to make the commitment to obtain and read a book on 9/11, but who wish to learn more, a ten-minute solution is available. It only takes a few minutes to view video on the Internet of the collapse of Building 7, the 47 story skyscraper located immediately north of the WTC complex about 300 feet from the North Tower.
Viewers will note the almost vertical collapse of the building. Only controlled demolitions have achieved vertical collapses of upright steel structures.

After viewing the video, many will agree with Dan Rather who said on CBS News that very evening that the collapse of Building 7 was "reminiscent of those pictures we've all seen too much on television before when a building was destroyed by well placed dynamite to knock it down." [14]

In addition, viewers may like to put the remaining time to good use by screening the 17 slides that make up Jim Hoffman's slide show presentation regarding Building 7's collapse. [15]

How did it happen that the nearly instant collapse of Building 7 involving the simultaneous destruction of its 58 perimeter steel columns and 25 core steel columns, all fireproofed, could have been disappeared so efficiently down the memory hole. As Jim Hoffman noted, the collapse of Building 7 did not even require a NOVA/Discovery Channel - style public relations campaign as explanation. Building 7 became a footnote, largely ignored by the public as well as the 9/11 Commission.

The Connection Between the Collapse of Building 7 and the Twin Towers

Once viewers are satisfied that Building 7 came down as a result of a controlled demolition, they may well ask whether its destruction entails that the Twin Towers also came down through similar means, and not because of the impact of the planes and the resulting fires. The question is critical because as Jim Hoffman argues, if the destruction of the Twin Towers (plus Building 7) were caused by demolition, the official story collapses since Osama Bin Laden did not have the means to demolish the buildings from within. "Demolition is an all-or-nothing proposition: There is no plausible deniability."[16]

Researcher Eric Hufschmid argues for a logical connection between the collapse of Building 7 and the Twin Towers and deduces that the only theory that makes sense is that the same group, which was responsible for bringing down Building 7, also brought down the Twin Towers. According to Hufschmid, anyone who suspects Building 7 was brought down by explosives "would have to conclude that explosives were used in the towers."[17]

Such a connection is controversial since it effectively indicts the U.S. government for responsibility for 9/11. That is one reason that Jim Hoffman theorizes that WTC owner Larry Silverstein went on TV to admit that he and the NYC Chief of Police together agreed to "pull the building" with "pull" being slang for bringing the building down by means of controlled demolition. He believes that Silverstein, in an attempt to confuse the issue and to quell suspicion, was implicitly arguing that the issue of Building 7 was separate and distinct and had nothing to do with the collapse of the Twin Towers.[18]

However, that may be, David Ray Griffin believes that evidence points to the possibility that the 9/11 conspiracy involved U.S. government officials as well as outside parties, possibly WTC owner Larry Silverstein.[19]

Why Was Building 7 Destroyed?

Since no serious investigation was permitted, researchers have been forced to speculate about the motives for including WTC 7 in the 9/11 destruction. Sufficient shock and awe had already been generated by the day's events, so it wasn't necessary to add the destruction of Building 7 to the mayhem.

On the contrary, its destruction through an all-too-evident controlled demolition would only prove to be an inexplicable embarrassment since a plane didn't hit the building. Two motivations that seem the most promising to explore are: a. destruction of evidence and b. insurance payouts to owner Larry Silverstein.

WTC 7 housed an emergency command center on the 23rd floor built in 1998 during Mayor Giuliani's tenure at a cost of $15 million. I join many in the 9/11 inquiry movement who find it plausible that this fire and wind-resistant unit housed the command center for the destruction of the Twin Towers as well as a homing device bringing the planes to their targets.[20] Many think that the building was brought down to destroy the equipment and the computers involved in the conspiracy.

Others have noted that Building 7 also contained offices of the Securities and Exchange Commission including files for approximately three to four thousand cases, including one that may have demonstrated the relationship between Citigroup and the WorldCom bankruptcy.

While destruction of the evidence has a strong appeal, I suspect that it was not the primary motive. For one thing, if the conspirators required that evidence needed to be destroyed in this way, I suspect they would have planned to bring the building down well before 5:20 PM.

Much more interesting as a line of investigation, it seems to me, is the insurance payout to Larry Silverstein. According to author Don Paul, Silverstein Properties won an $861 million award from Industrial Risk Insurers to rebuild on the site of WTC 7. Silverstein Properties' estimated investment in WTC 7 was $386 million, netting a profit of about $500 million.[21]

David Ray Griffin also suggests that Silverstein's insurance considerations should be investigated as a motive in the destruction of the WTC buildings. Griffin points out that on April 26, 2001, Silverstein had taken out a lease on the WTC and wound up with a multibillion-dollar settlement when a federal jury ruled in December 2004 that the attacks constituted two occurrences.

More important perhaps, is that according to court filings, Silverstein had a plan to seek a huge profit from a small and brief investment in the World Trade Center apart from his claim for a double payment for the destruction of the Twin Towers. Griffin quotes court documents to the effect that Silverstein had only $14 million invested in the insurance deal for the Twin Towers (compared to 50 times as much by his lenders) through limited liability investment vehicles.
The deal was structured to enable Silverstein to "walk away" from the lease if the buildings were destroyed, ending up with a balance of $1 billion. Griffin surmises that if the allegations are confirmed, "then it provides circumstantial support for those who believe that Silverstein took out the insurance with the knowledge that the buildings *would* be destroyed." (Emphasis in original) Griffin believes that consideration of the "destruction of the WTC as an inside job cannot be ruled out *a priori* because there would have been no conceivable motive."[22]

The Logical Connection

What is the logical connection between the collapse of the Twin Towers on the morning of 9/11 and the 5:20 PM collapse of Building 7?

Eric Hufschmid begins by pointing to two possibilities: either the conspirators decided to bring down Building 7 **after** they saw the Twin Towers collapse or they prepared a demolition scenario **beforehand**. [22]

Hufschmid first dispenses with the possibility that the conspirators took measures to bring down Building 7 **after** they saw the Twin Towers collapse.

Such a scenario would require that several people quickly come together and arrange to bring explosives into the area, plan and place the charges, a process that usually takes several days or more. They would have to manage countless details, including the removal of all Building 7 personnel and the control of access to the crime scene. All this would have had to be undertaken spontaneously in the hectic time between 10 AM and 5:20 PM.

Hufschmid concludes that it is most likely that plans for the demolition of WTC –7 were prepared **before** 9/11. He theorizes that explosives were set in place in good time and similarly the mechanics of setting off the demolition were arranged beforehand. In this case, Hufschmid argues, logic and/or common sense suggest that the same group of conspirators organized the destruction of all three towers.

Could Building 7 Stand Alone as a Case of Solo Collapse?

What would happen, Hufschmid asks, if, on 9/11, airplanes hit the towers, but they didn't collapse? Wouldn't it be suspicious if Building 7 had collapsed from fires smaller than those in the Towers? Might not the firemen "respond that fires *do not cause steel buildings to collapse*? … Scientists and engineers would want to analyze the steel beams to see how fire did what no fire had done before." Hufschmid argues that it would not be safe to destroy Building 7 unless the towers collapse first. "After the towers collapse, the collapse of Building 7 would appear to be just another weird event of that day's bizarre disasters." (Italics in original)

Hufschmid goes on to argue that there is likely to have been coordination between the people who set the explosives and the alleged hijackers;[23] or that the conspirators had some kind of control over the hijackers since it wouldn't make sense to prepare the explosives and then depend on the hijackers to follow through on their own. "What if the hijackers decide to switch from hitting the World Trade Center to hitting the U.S. Capitol... or they miss the towers and hit some other building?"

"An even more likely problem is that the hijackers get control of the aircraft...and then the FAA realizes that something is seriously wrong. The FAA contacts the military, and the military sends up a plane to investigate..."

As David Ray Griffin and others have pointed out, military jet interceptions of wayward passenger jets is a routine occurrence. In the year before 9/11, from September 2000 through June 2001, there were 67 such interceptions, [24] but there were none on 9/11/01. (If the major media had chosen to make public this information about these routine military interceptions, and their absence on 9/11, suspicion of U.S. government involvement would undoubtedly be more widespread.)

Hufschmid concludes that the plot to destroy Building 7 required the cooperation of the FAA and/or the military. In addition, the conspirators would need to have control of the investigations and to do so they would have to destroy the evidence that remained in the ruins of the buildings and the rubble, a crime.

Thus, the conspirators would have to have "influence over our government." In the event, U.S. government control over Ground Zero led to the hasty destruction of the rubble and the removal of most of the remaining steel to be destroyed in Indian and Chinese blast furnaces. In addition, FEMA investigators were prevented from free access to Ground Zero and to the evidence.

Once we conclude that Building 7 was brought down by a controlled demolition, it follows that the same group of conspirators also caused the collapse of the Twin Towers. It is also clear that such a conspiracy could not have been undertaken had it not been intimately connected to the highest levels of the U.S. military, in other words, the U.S. government.

9/11, AN INSIDE JOB? (A REVIEW ESSAY BASED ON DAVID RAY GRIFFIN'S RESEARCH)

by Ronald Bleier

June 2005

Editor's Notes

This essay was originally conceived as the first of two parts. I changed plans and focused my follow-up article on the No Planes on 9/11 theory. Nevertheless, I also incorporated some of the issues I had originally intended, especially the attack on the Pentagon.

My epigraph quotes President George W. Bush's speech two months after 9/11 at the U.N. when he explicitly warned his audience against adopting conspiracy theories. I still haven't figured out whether he was signaling concern that his false flag would be exposed, or if he was merely employing his trademark smirk.

***

The Air Defense Stand-Down

> *We must speak the truth about terror. Let us never tolerate outrageous conspiracy theories concerning the attacks of September the 11th, malicious lies that attempt to shift the blame away from the terrorists themselves, away from the guilty.*

- President G.W. Bush to the U.N. General Assembly, 11/10/01

W

as 9/11 an inside job? David Ray Griffin addresses this question in two books that critically examine the official account of the events of 9/11. Griffin's books are masterpieces of concise compilations of the available plausible evidence suggesting that the attacks must have resulted from complicity at the highest levels of the United States government. This review essay treats both books as a unit, summarizes some of his most important findings, and includes relevant material from other researchers.

Like most Americans, Griffin, a retired professor of Philosophy at the Claremont School of Theology (California), at first viewed critics of the Bush administration's account as crackpots.

It seemed to him that conspiracy theories on this subject were below the threshold of possibility. In the 18 months following 9/11, he had not looked at any of the evidence challenging the government's theory –- that the attacks were the responsibility of 19 Arab hijackers led by Osama Bin Laden. It seemed to him, as he writes in his introduction, "beyond belief that the Bush administration – even the Bush administration -- would do such a heinous thing." (*The New Pearl Harbor*, [NPH], xvii-xviii)

But in the spring of 2003, a colleague prodded him to look at researcher Paul Thompson's 9/11 timeline which is strictly limited to mainstream sources.[25] Griffin was "surprised, even amazed, to see how much evidence he had found that points to the conclusion that the Bush administration did indeed intentionally allow the attacks of 9/11 to happen." Griffin began to look at the work of Nafeez Ahmed, an independent researcher in England, whose book "directly challenges the accepted wisdom about 9/11 which is that it resulted from a breakdown within and among our intelligence agencies.

Ahmed, like Thompson, suggests that the attacks must have resulted from complicity in high places, not merely from incompetence in lower places." Taken together, Griffin concludes, Ahmed and Thompson "provided a strong *prima facie* case for this contention." Because the work of Ahmed and Thompson were not likely to reach many American readers, and because of the U.S. media's failure to provide an in-depth investigation, Griffin decided to write a magazine article which grew into his first book, *The New Pearl Harbor*. (NPH, xviii-xix)[26]

Griffin's Title: The New Pearl Harbor

Griffin explains that the title of his first book, *The New Pearl Harbor* (NPH), alludes, in part, simply to the pointed references to Pearl Harbor that were made in the immediate wake of the 9/11 attacks. For example, President Bush wrote in his diary that evening: "The Pearl Harbor of the 21st century took place today."

Henry Kissinger in an online post on 9/11 wrote that he hoped that the U.S. government's response "will end the way that the attack on Pearl Harbor ended – with the destruction of the system that is responsible for it." (NPH, xi)

The title also has a deeper meaning. Griffin cites a commentary by John Pilger suggesting that the events of 9/11 presented an opportunity that was predicted in 2000 by soon-to-be top Bush administration officials. The neoconservative Project for the New American Century September 2000 document, "Rebuilding America's Defenses," written or subscribed to by such figures as Dick Cheney, Donald Rumsfeld, and Paul Wolfowitz, reasoned that the changes they had in mind for the direction of U.S. policy would be difficult to achieve "absent some catastrophic and catalyzing event — like a new Pearl Harbor."

(NPH, xi) Griffin's title is a reference to the Bush administration's opportunistic use of the 9/11 terror events to embark on a plan of "aggressive imperialism" that has led to two wars, to sharp increases in military spending, a dramatic shift towards a national security state and a sustained attack on civil liberties. (NPH, xii)

Why a Second Book on 9/11?

As his title indicates, Professor Griffin's second book on 9/11, THE 9/11 COMMISSION REPORT: OMISSIONS AND DISTORTIONS (O&D), is intended as a response to the *9/11 Commission Report* (July 2004), which gained immediate mainstream popularity and credibility. *The New Pearl Harbor* can be read as an investigation into an extraordinary crime perpetrated by the U.S. government on its own people, and *Omissions and Distortions* as an expose of the cover-up of the crime (although each book contains elements of both).

Readers open to the message of *The New Pearl Harbor* may divide as to the implications over the level of the Bush administration's complicity in the terror events.

Some may take the view that the success of the attacks was due merely to administration incompetence, combined with understandable mistakes, some foreknowledge and a willingness to let it happen, roughly the LIHOP school (Let It Happen On Purpose). Although Griffin presents considerable evidence supporting the stronger conclusions of the MIHOP school (Made It Happen On Purpose), many readers may assume that that evidence could be explained away.

However, readers of Griffin's second book (especially after having read the first) are more likely to find that it is difficult to escape the conclusion that the White House must have been deeply involved in planning and executing the 9/11 attacks. The difference is that readers can see that although the 9/11 Commission had the opportunity to rebut the allegations summarized in the first book, they simply ignored most of them.

The strength and effectiveness of Griffin's work comes in part from his mastery of the subject, the depth of his research, his brilliant organizational ability and the clarity with which he presents extremely detailed and complicated information. Those who agree with the author's fundamental assumption, that there is a strong *prima facie* case for critically examining the official story, are likely to experience a sense of relief that an independent and competent authority is finally pulling back the immense curtain of fog behind which the terror attacks are still hidden. Griffin's work empowers and helps to unify his readers who were confused and isolated by the shock of the attacks and their aftermath.

A hallmark of Griffin's writing is his measured language. He is as precise as possible, cautiously never going beyond known facts and reasonable common-sense deductions. In *The New Pearl Harbor*, while he presents information that could plausibly suggest the highest possible level of official complicity, Griffin pretty much limits himself to calling for an independent investigation of the many troubling and substantial issues raised by the 9/11 events.

In his second book, published after it became clear to Griffin and many other skeptics that there was to be no credible independent inquiry into the 9/11 events, the tone is often stronger and Griffin goes as far as speaking of the *9/11 Report's* "audacious lies," in addition to detailing its often breathtaking "omissions and distortions."

Nevertheless, for the most part, even in his second book, he conservatively limits himself to the conclusions that can fairly be drawn from the available evidence. Again, Griffin shrinks from coming right out and accusing the Bush administration of planning and executing the 9/11 attacks. Rather he concludes his inquiry with a question: Why would the people in charge of writing the 9/11 Commission Report engage in such extraordinary deception if they were not trying to cover up very high crimes? (O&D, 291)

***

Griffin begins *The New Pearl Harbor* by examining some of the commonly accepted notions of the events of 9/11/2001. Critics claim that not one of the planes that hit the Twin Towers and the Pentagon should have reached its target, let alone all three of them. In the normal course of events, military jets would have intercepted and if necessary, shot down the errant airliners before they reached their targets. There are troubling aspects with Flight 93, the plane that reportedly went down in Shankesville, Pennsylvania. Skeptics cite testimony and other reasons to think that the U.S. Air Force shot it down. Moreover, the official story about the collapse of the Twin Towers and Building 7 of the World Trade Center is not credible. The commonly accepted view is that the Twin Towers collapsed due to the impact of the planes and the resulting fires and Building 7 from fire alone, but skeptics believe that they collapsed because of preplanned controlled demolitions. Finally, there are disturbing questions about the behavior of President Bush and the Secret Service that day that could point to guilty foreknowledge of a U.S. government conspiracy. (NPH, 3)

The Apparent Air Defense Stand-down

Remarkably little attention has been paid in the mainstream press to the simple question of why the most expensive and technologically advanced air defense system in the world was unable to protect the U.S. homeland for almost two hours after the first indications of trouble in the skies. How did it happen that 19 Arab alleged hijackers with minimal flying skills were able to take over four planes and successfully pilot them through heavily trafficked air corridors on illegal flight plans without routine military interception? Is it conceivable that the U.S. did not have the timely information required to prevent the attacks?

Flight 11 Strikes the North Tower at 8:46 AM

As early as 8:13 or 8:14 AM the FAA registered the loss of radio contact with American Airlines Flight 11 and the loss of transponder signal at 8:15. (O&D, 155) [27] Under normal conditions, the military would have been notified within minutes and under standard operating procedures, the wayward passenger plane would have been intercepted by 8:24 or 8:30 at the latest. Such interceptions are routine. The FAA reported that in a 10-month period before 9/11, between September 2000 and June 2001 there were 67 military interceptions of passenger planes. (O&D, 140)

The issue is complicated by Bush administration's attempts to confuse the issue. On the Sunday following 9/11, Vice President Cheney, on *Meet the Press* (9/16/01) implied that a presidential order was required for interceptions as well as shoot-downs. (NPH, p.6) Interceptions are routine procedures whereby military jets are scrambled or diverted from training or patrol flights to communicate visually, if necessary, with wayward planes and bring them to a correct course or escort them to an appropriate airport.

These interceptions occur more than once a week on average. Shoot downs are more extreme procedures generally requiring top-level authorization. General Richard Meyers, then Acting Chairman of the Joint Chiefs of Staff, in testimony to the Senate Armed Services Committee on September 13, also helped to confuse the issue when he implied incorrectly that fighters sent up to intercept aircraft could only do so if ordered by commanders at the highest level. (NPH, p.6)

In addition, such interceptions normally occur quickly. General Ralph Eberhart, the head of NORAD (the North American Aerospace Defense Command), explained in 2002, that "it takes about a minute" for the FAA to contact NORAD, "after which NORAD can scramble jets "within a matter of minutes to anywhere in the United States."

According to the U.S. Air Force website, "an F-15 routinely "goes from 'scramble order to 29,000 ft. in only 2.5 minutes, after which it can fly 1850 miles per hour." (O&D, 140)

Flight 175 Strikes the South Tower at 9:03 AM

United Airlines Flight 175 left Boston at 8:14. By 8:42, its radio and transponder went off, and it veered off course. By then controllers knew that the earlier flight had been hijacked and they would surely have been ready to contact the military. In fact, in the second version of the official story, they notified NORAD, a minute later, at 8:43. NORAD should have had fighters intercepting this plane by 8:53, and by this time, seven minutes after the first plane hit the South Tower, should have been ready to shoot down the second hijacked plane if necessary. (NPH, 7)

Another disturbing feature connected with Flight 175 is that at 8:55 AM a public announcement broadcast inside the South Tower indicated that the building was secure so that people could return to their offices.

Researcher Paul Thompson asks: why weren't people warned? Griffin suggests that the implication is that someone other than the hijackers wanted to insure that there would be a sufficient number of casualties to deliver the shock and awe the conspirators required. (NPH, 7)

Since the second plane hit the WTC 17 minutes after the first, none of the possible explanations for the failure to intercept the first plane -- inattentive air traffic controllers, pilots at military bases not at full alert, or the assumption that the plane's aberrant behavior did not mean that it had been hijacked – could apply. (NPH, 7-8).

Helpful background information on the significance of transponder signals is provided in journalist and 9/11 critic Michael Rupert's *Crossing the Rubicon*.

Ruppert explains that all commercial airliners are equipped with transponders —devices that identify the altitude and position of planes by means of radio signals to air traffic controllers (ATCs). When transponders go off, the plane can still be tracked in two dimensions, but the ATC can no longer pinpoint its altitude. At that point, the system is in emergency status and the offending plane appears on the consoles of all the local ATCs. Ruppert goes on to quote from the statement of a pilot, Michael Guillaume, who explains that such a plane...

> is now a hazard to air navigation, and the controller's primary function of separating planes is now in jeopardy...If in addition to losing communication and transponder the flight starts to deviate from its last clearance, the whole system is in an emergency condition. Alarms all over the country would be going off...

> So we know that the traffic control system would be in panic mode within two or three minutes of the initial events.... The odds are that many flights would be on patrol just offshore. It would be most improbable that even one commercial flight could go [astray] more than ten minutes without being intercepted....

> Interceptions are routine daily occurrences. The fact that they didn't happen under extreme provocation raises some serious questions...[30]

Even more pointed information about the consequences of interruption of transponder signal comes from French 9/11 researcher Thierry Meyssan. He writes, "turning off the transponder, under the conditions that prevailed that day, would have been the best way of raising an alert."

> The procedures are very strict in the case of a problem with a transponder, both on civilian and military aircraft. The FAA regulations describe exactly how to proceed when a transponder is not functioning properly: the control tower should enter radio contact at once with the pilot and, if it fails, immediately warn the military who would then send fighters to establish visual contact with the crew. [see FAA regulations: http://faa.gov/ATpubs]

> The interruption of a transponder also directly sets off an alert with the military body responsible for air defenses of the United States and Canada, NORAD.
> The transponder is the plane's identity card. An aircraft that disposes of this identity card is IMMEDIATELY monitored, AUTOMATICALLY. "If an object has not been identified in less than two minutes or appears suspect, it is considered ... an eventual threat. Unidentified planes, planes in distress and planes we suspect are being used for illegal activities can then be intercepted by a fighter from NORAD. [NORAD spokesman: http://www.airforce,dnd.ca/athomedocs/athome1e_f.htm])28

With this information in mind, we come back to the question of why the planes that struck the Twin Towers weren't intercepted. In the immediate aftermath of 9/11, the Bush administration apparently wasn't prepared with a convincing answer to this fundamental question and in the end, three versions of the official response were required. The first version was enunciated two days later when General Richard Myers, at his previously scheduled confirmation hearing, testified to the Senate that the order to scramble aircraft "to the best of my knowledge, was [given] after the Pentagon was struck." (NPH, 8).

The problem with this first version, later confirmed by NORAD spokesman, Major Mike Snyder, and indirectly by no less than Vice President Cheney,29 is that it seemed to imply that a government-ordered stand-down order had been arranged. Researchers Israel and Bykov, correctly label Myers's testimony as "disastrous" for precisely that reason and the official story was quickly modified.30 The next day CBS evening news floated the new cover story. "In the new script, fighter jets from Otis and Langley Air Force Bases did try, but failed, to intercept the hijacked planes." 31 This became the second version of the official story that took more formal shape when NORAD published its timeline of 9/11 events on September 18th, 2001.

Thus, was born the second version of the official story. The clear purpose of NORAD's September 18th document was to exculpate the military from responsibility by suggesting that human error and understandable mistakes prevented military jets from arriving on time. But Griffin speaks for the critical consensus when he writes that there is good reason to assume the truth that no fighters were dispatched until after the Pentagon was hit at 9:38. Griffin argues that Myers and Snyder were in a position to know what happened on 9/11 and "it is hard to suppose that they would have fabricated this account since it certainly did not make the U.S. military look good." (O&D, 143)[32]

The 9/11 Commission's Explanation

In his June 2004 testimony to the 9/11 Commission, General Richard Myers testified that our air defenses failed in part because we were situated to defend against an external rather than an internal threat. "We did not have the situational awareness inward because we did not have the radar coverage." (O&D, 260)

The issue of radar coverage plays a key role in the Commission's explanation for the inability of the military to prevent the first plane from striking the North Tower.
The 9/11 Commission presents a tortuous account whereby the military was not informed that there was a problem with Flight 11 until 8:38.

As noted above, had standard operating procedures been followed, the military would have been appraised at 8:15 or at the latest at 8:20, in plenty of time to intercept Flight 11 before it struck the North Tower at 8:46. Yet, according to the Commission account, even at 8:38, Battle Commander Colonel Robert Marr at NEADS merely ordered fighter pilots at Otis AFB to battle stations. [33]

Then, according to the Commission, he placed an 8-minute telephone call to Major General Larry Arnold, at NORAD's U.S. Continental Region in Florida, to seek authorization to scramble airplanes. By these means, the Commission generated the scramble order time of 8:46, just 40 seconds before Flight 11 struck the North Tower. (O&D, 165)[34]

But Griffin suspects that the Commission may have felt that the story of an eight-minute phone call merely to seek authorization to scramble planes might not seem plausible. Griffin teases out of the *Commission Report* an "implicit" reason for the delay: namely that the military didn't have at its disposal radar capable of spotting the wayward Boeing 767 on its way to Manhattan. Griffin quotes the *Commission Report*, which claims that after Flight 11's transponder was turned off, "NEADS personnel spent the next ten minutes [from 8:38 to 8:48] searching their radar scopes for the primary radar return... Shortly after 8:50 while NEADS personnel were still trying to locate the flight, word reached them that a plane had hit the WTC." (O&D, 166-167)

However, as Griffin points out, "This account suggests that a loss of transponder makes it virtually impossible for the U.S. military to track airplanes."

If that were true, "Soviet airplanes during the Cold War could have avoided detection by simply turning off their transponders." Griffin found no sign in the *9/11 Commission Report* that this obvious objection was raised. Instead, he writes, "the Commission apparently accepted and wrote down with a straight face, the assertion that NEADS personnel spent several minutes trying to find Flight 11 on their radar screens... But this statement grossly misrepresents the capabilities of the U.S. military's radar systems. For one thing the military radar system, unlike civilian radar, does not need the transponder to tell the plane's altitude." (O&D, 167)

Griffin cites French critic Thierry Meyssan, who points to the Pentagon's own websites, which imply that it possesses "several very sophisticated radar monitoring systems, incomparable with the civilian systems." The website for one of these systems, called PAVE PAWS,[35] says that it is "capable of detecting and monitoring a great number of targets that would be consistent with a massive SLBM [Submarine Launched Ballistic Missile] attack." Griffin surmises that the "PAVE PAWS system is surely not premised on the assumption that ... SLBMs would have transponders." (O&D, 166-167)

Thierry Meyssan details some of the capabilities of PAVE PAWS. It is used, he writes, to detect and track objects difficult to pick up such as missiles flying at very low altitudes. PAVE PAWS misses NOTHING occurring in North American airspace. "The radar system is capable of detecting and monitoring a great number of targets that would be consistent with a massive SLBM attack. The system is capable of rapidly discriminating between vehicle types, calculating their launch and impact points," [http://www.pavepaws.org/ and http://www.fas.org/spp/military/program/track/pave paws.htm] [36] By accepting General Richard Myers's testimony as fact, and by not including an adequate description of U.S. radar monitoring capabilities consistent with the information on U.S. government websites, Griffin concludes that the 9/11 Commission, which he calls the Kean-Zelikow Commission,[37] is guilty of a major distortion. (O&D, 167)

Bush's Behavior on 9/11

"It was an interesting day."
- President Bush, recalling 9/11

Skeptics of the official story of 9/11 have raised disturbing questions about the president's behavior during the course of the attacks. His actions and reactions were not what would be expected if he and his aides were taken by surprise. The official version of his movements and of what he knew and when he knew it is in some places contradictory, contrary to known facts, and otherwise incomprehensible unless one assumes foreknowledge on the part of his administration.

At 8:35 AM, on the morning of 9/11/01, President Bush's motorcade left his hotel and headed for a photo opportunity at Booker Elementary School in Sarasota, Florida.[38] According to spokesman Ari Fleischer at a White House press conference that same evening, it wasn't until President Bush arrived at the school just before 9 AM that he was told that a plane had flown into the WTC. (NPH, p. 57) It's difficult to believe that the president didn't know about the first plane strike before he arrived at the school since millions became aware of the first plane crashing into the WTC by 8:48. Most people would assume that the president would be among the first to be informed. (NPH, 57)

Paul Thompson cites a *Washington Times* account that Bush was told that a plane had crashed in NYC while he was on his way to the school [between 8:46-8:55 AM].[39] Photographer Eric Draper, riding in another car in the motorcade with Press Secretary Ari Fleischer, overheard Fleischer say on a cell phone, "Oh my God, I don't believe it. A plane just hit the World Trade Center." [Between 8:46-8:55 AM].

In yet another account, the president didn't learn of the attack until he arrived at the school at 8:55 when Karl Rove rushed up to him, took him aside in a corridor and told him. According to photographer Eric Draper, Bush replied, "What a horrible accident!" [Between 8:55-9:00 a.m.][40]

A report about CIA Director George Tenet raises more questions relevant to the president's knowledge and actions that morning. A few minutes after 8:46 a.m., Tenet was told of the crash while at breakfast with former Senator David Boren in Washington D.C. Boren noted that Tenet was told that an airplane attacked the WTC. Tenet said to Boren, "You know, this has bin Laden's fingerprints all over it." Thompson asks: "Why is Bush supposedly under the impression the crash was an accident well after Tenet has been told it was an attack?" Thompson wonders if Tenet has tried to communicate with Bush at this time. [8:50 a.m.]

By the time the first pictures of the burning North Tower were broadcast, the FAA, NORAD, the NMCC[41], the Pentagon, the White House, the Secret Service and Canada's Strategic Command all knew that three commercial planes had been hijacked. (NPH, 59) The overriding question hanging over Bush's actions at the school is: why did he decide to maintain his schedule in the face of a national emergency?

Skeptics suggest that the session at the Booker School may have been staged in order to provide the president with an alibi to justify his inaction during the attacks and to indirectly explain the lack of an effective U.S. military air defense. If the president was unaware of a national emergency, that would explain why he couldn't coordinate the military response to the attacks.

It would also explain why Vice President Cheney had to take over many of his emergency duties.[42] Evidence that the president downplayed knowledge that a terror attack was underway is provided by the testimony of Gwen Tose Rigell, Principal of the Booker School, who said:

> "I actually heard the first plane had hit from the president, and he said that a plane had hit the World Trade Center and that it was a commercial plane,' says Rigell. 'He said but we're going to go on, and in my mind, I had created this picture of a plane knocking off some bricks on the corner of the World Trade Center.'"[43]

Bush's Town Hall Meetings

President Bush addressed the question of his actions that morning when he responded to questions at two town hall meetings in December 2001 and January 2002. In his December 2001 Town Hall meeting in Orlando, Florida, President Bush responded to a third grader named Jordan, who had asked him: "How did you feel when you heard about the terrorist attack?" President Bush responded:

> Well, Jordan, you're not going to believe what state I was in when I heard about the terrorist attack. I was in Florida. And my Chief of Staff, Andy Card -- actually, I was in a classroom talking about a reading program that works. I was sitting outside the classroom waiting to go in, and I saw an airplane hit the tower -- the TV was obviously on. And I used to fly myself, and I said, well, there's one terrible pilot. I said it must have been a horrible accident.
>
> But I was whisked off there; I didn't have much time to think about it. And I was sitting in the classroom, and Andy Card, my Chief of Staff, who is sitting over here, walked in and said, "A second plane has hit the tower, America is under attack." 44

Bush's version is problematical on at least two counts. For one thing, he could not have seen the first plane hit the WTC on live TV because the only known video of the first strike was not broadcast until the next day.

Secondly, 9/11 skeptics believe that not only did he learn of the strike before he arrived at the school but that he and his party, in all likelihood, knew very well, unlike most Americans, that the strike was not a "horrible accident," but was rather a deliberate act of terror.[45]

In addition, Griffin and others suggest that Bush's statement that he saw the first plane hit the tower could suggest foreknowledge of the attacks. (NPH, 62).

> *I was sitting outside the classroom waiting to go in, and I saw an airplane hit the tower -- the TV was obviously on.*

Before he entered the classroom for the reading lesson, Bush went into a "hold," a room at the school prepared especially for the president and his staff complete with TV and communications equipment. Perhaps it was then that Bush saw the first strike when he said he did if a secret government video of the crash was available.[46] It's notable that Bush felt he had to add the phrase, "the TV was obviously on," as if he realized that he was divulging privileged information.

Indirect Evidence

There are a number of indirect indications that the president and key aides must have been aware that America was under attack when the first plane hit the WTC at 8:46 (if not twenty minutes earlier). We have already noted that by the time the first pictures of the burning North Tower were broadcast at 8:48, the FAA, NORAD, the NMCC, the Pentagon, the White House, the Secret Service and Canada's Strategic Command all knew that three commercial planes had been hijacked. Presumably, that is how Bush knew that the plane that struck the first Tower was a commercial aircraft when he spoke to Principal Rigell before 9 a.m. and thus he must have been aware the U.S. was under attack.

Another indirect indication of real-time knowledge of critical information by the White House is Vice President Cheney's perhaps inadvertent comment on *Meet the Press* on Sept 16, 2001, when he said," The Secret Service has an arrangement with the FAA. They had open lines after the WTC was…"(at which point he stopped himself.) (NPH, 57)

Cheney's apparent admission of the connection raises enormous difficulties for the official story not only because it challenges the White House version of the president's behavior. If the Secret Service was in the loop as early as 8:46, it's necessarily the case that the military was informed of developing threats to the South Tower (9:03 a.m.) and the Pentagon (9:38 a.m.) as well as issues with flight 93, apparently downed in Pennsylvania shortly after 10 AM.

More information about the deployment of Secret Service personnel comes from Mike Ruppert who points to a footnote in the *9/11 Commission Report* which cites a Secret Service agent speaking to his "counterpart" at the FAA HQ in Washington D.C. "shortly after the second attack in New York." With his background as a Los Angeles police officer, Ruppert guesses that the "counterpart" in question might have been a Secret Service agent stationed at FAA HQ.[47] In that case, it would indicate that the Secret Service, and thus the president's party, knew in real-time everything that the FAA knew about the developing national security emergency on the morning of 9/11 beginning perhaps as early as 8:13 a.m.

Indirect evidence that the president and his top aides were aware that the military was called into action as early as 8:37 a.m. comes from the 9/11 Commission itself. *The Report* gives 8:37 a.m. as the time Boston flight controllers notified the military that AA Flight 11 was hijacked, that the plane was seriously off course and headed toward NYC.

Shortly afterward, according to the Commission, jets were scrambled. In that case, it would be imperative to contact the president if only to inform him that it might be necessary to order a shoot down.

Even 8:37 a.m. would have been remarkably late for the military to be informed about problems that morning with a commercial airliner off course. Paul Thompson emphasizes that 8:37 is 24 minutes after radio contact was lost at 8:13 A.M, 17 minutes after the transponder signal was lost and the flight went far off course, and approximately 13 minutes after the hijackers in the cockpit clearly stated that the plane had been hijacked at 8:24 A. M. (8:37 a.m.)

More indirect evidence about Secret Service capabilities comes from President Bush's Counterterrorism advisor, Richard Clarke who wrote that the "Secret Service had a system that allowed them to see what the FAA's radar was seeing."[48] This means that the Secret Service was in a position to know that the FAA was in crisis mode as early as 8:13 or 8:20 a.m. in which case many would assume that the president in Florida would have been informed. (O&D, 48)

There is also information from Laura Brown, the Deputy in charge of Public Affairs at FAA headquarters that the National Military Command Center's (NMCC) threat teleconference [49] may have been set up as early as 8:20 or 8:25. But this early time is in dispute. *The 9/11 Commission Report* informs us that this Pentagon-initiated teleconference did not begin until 9:29. But the sole support for this belated start is some anonymous person at the Pentagon. Laura Brown at first gave 8:20 or 8:25 as the starting time to journalist and 9/11 critic Tom Flocco. Such a time would be reasonable since it was determined that AA Flight 11 was hijacked at 8:13, 8:20, or 8:24.

But after conferring with her superiors, Brown changed her story, revising her initial time to around 8:45, about the time that the North Tower was struck.

Even this later time would indicate that the lead Secret Service agent as well as other top White House officials traveling with the president knew of an emergency situation while the motorcade was still on its way to the elementary school. (O&D, 186-187)

Ignoring the Threat to the President?

Most "astounding," writes Griffin, about the presidential party's movements that morning is that the secret service seemed to ignore a possible threat to the president since it would have been logical to assume that he would have been one of the intended targets.

Indeed, after viewing TV coverage of the second plane striking the WTC, one Secret Service agent reportedly said, "We're out of here," and yet the president remained at the school for another half hour. By contrast, Griffin notes, at the same time in Washington D.C., Rice and Cheney were moved to secure bunkers. (NPH, 59) In the end, Bush didn't leave the school until 9:34, shortly after he delivered a talk to the nation exactly as previously scheduled at 9:29 am.[50] (*Terror Timeline*, 418).

Griffin goes on for almost two pages describing Bush's leisurely behavior at the school, even after the president was notified at 9:05 a.m. of the second attack. Griffin quotes intelligence expert and author James Bamford who writes that Bush "appeared uninterested in further details. He never asked if there had been any additional threats, where the attacks were coming from, how to best protect the country from further attacks…" (NPH, 59). Viewers of the Michael Moore film, *Fahrenheit 911*, saw the president remain seated in the classroom for minutes after he was notified of the second strike on the WTC.

Instead, as Griffin (once again quoting Bamford) notes, while the situation at the WTC was becoming increasingly desperate with people jumping to their deaths, the president was listening to the children reading a story called "The Pet Goat."
"A-girl-got-a-pet-goat. But-the-goat-did–some-things-that-made-the-girl's-dad-mad." After the lesson, according to Bill Sammon, an author generally sympathetic to the president, Bush "openly stretched out the moment," giving a pep talk to the students, answering questions about education, chatting with the children, posing for pictures with the classroom teacher and in general appearing as the "dawdler in chief." (NPH, 60-61)

Griffin finds it "amazing" that "perhaps stung by the criticisms of the president's behavior, the White House put out a different account a year later" which had the president leaving the classroom within seconds of being told about the second attack at 9:05. Griffin notes that skeptics believe that the "White House was so confident that none of its lies about 9/11 would be challenged by the media that it felt safe telling this one even though it is flatly contradicted by Sammon's pro-Bush book[51] and by the video tape produced that day…" (NPH, 61)

After Bush's televised address to the nation at 9:29, the presidential party proceeded on their scheduled motorcade to the airport (NPH, 62), where they were presumably informed that the Pentagon had been struck at 9:38 and that Air Force One might come under terrorist attack.

Skeptics wonder why no military escort had been ordered by 9:55 a.m. when Air Force One took off. At that time as many as eleven aircraft were under suspicion of being hijacked. The implied question is once again, did the president and his aides "know that he was *not* a target?" (NPH, 62)

The Commission on the President's Behavior

In his book on the 9/11 Commission report, Griffin asserts that the Commission's treatment of the issues raised by the president's behavior is completely unsatisfactory.

For example, he finds that the Commission defends the president's dawdling at the school by arguing that the president's instinct was to project calm. Griffin notes that the Commission doesn't seem to have an opinion on whether such a response is satisfactory, or whether an appearance of calm was more important than getting himself and the students and school personnel out of harm's way, or even if, under the circumstances, a lack of calm would have been appropriate. (O&D, 41) The Commission at one point suggests that the Secret Service didn't think it imperative for Mr. Bush "to run out the door." Griffin wonders why the Commissioners didn't think to suggest that there would have been an option somewhere between 'runn[ing] out the door' and remaining at the school for another half hour." (O& D, 43)

On the issue of why air cover was not ordered, Griffin notes that not seeing to the protection of the president under such circumstances would seem to involve gross incompetence unless it was based on foreknowledge that the president would not be a target.

The Secret Service never did arrange for protection of the presidential motorcade and when Air Force One took off at 9:54, it did so without a military jet escort. Griffin notes that the Commission showed that it was aware of the issue but didn't see fit to ask the Secret Service why they didn't call for air cover. (O&D, 44)

Griffin writes that the Commission tried to answer the most publicized charge, namely that the president stayed away from Washington for so long that day because he was afraid. The Commission argues that this charge is unfair. However, Griffin emphasizes that this is the wrong question to ask about the president's behavior. The real issue is that neither the president nor any of his top aides seemed to have any fear "when they should have been very afraid." (O&D, 47)

The Denial of Presidential Knowledge

Griffin concludes his examination of the president's behavior with a section discussing the Commission's strong claim that "No one in the traveling party had any information during this time that other aircraft were hijacked or missing." Griffin argues that this "claim is essential. Without it, the decision to remain and continue reading the children's story could not have been rationalized." (O&D, 47) Griffin cites the Cheney and Clarke statements above to suggest that the Commission's "claim that the presidential party had no knowledge about other hijackings is, therefore almost certainly false. They couldn't say, 'We knew that the president was not in danger.' Griffin concludes: "The failure of the Kean-Zelikow Commission to point out this dilemma provides one of the many clues that it was dedicated to something other than revealing the truth about 9/11." (O&D, 48)

Here and in every single crucial aspect of the official story about 9/11, the case for Bush administration foreknowledge and the likelihood that the Bush administration was deeply involved in the planning and execution of the 9/11 attacks is immeasurably strengthened by the wholly unsatisfactory defense provided by the *9/11 Commission Report*. The manifest unwillingness of the authors of the *Report* to convincingly address the most pressing and obvious questions about the official version is in itself a tacit and powerful admission of guilt. It's reasonable to assume that had there been an innocent explanation for the president and his party's extraordinary actions and responses that morning, the Commission would have been eager to lay it out. Instead, as Griffin and other researchers have concluded, no such explanation has been forthcoming with the result that the public is forced to make its own deductions. □

WEBSTER TARPLEY AND ROGUE NETWORKS

by Ronald Bleier

February 2006

Editor's Notes

I wrote the following brief essay in response to Webster Tarpley's remarks claiming that a "rogue network" forced President George W. Bush and Vice President Dick Cheney to "launch a war on civilization." I was totally gob smacked to see Tarpley going off on this preposterous notion of some mysterious, alien organization directing U.S. imperialist adventures. It seemed a stunning lack of understanding of how things work in the real world. All the evidence I saw showed the White House to be evil and powerful enough without the aid of an even stronger, overriding invisible power.

Among other things, Tarpley's theory is evidence of the disarray and confusion not uncommon when false flags are not exposed. In the few examples when such operations are exposed, such as in the case of the aborted Northwoods plan (1962), there is little such pressure to posit a rogue network.

***

H

ave others noticed that Webster Tarpley, author of *9/11, Synthetic Terror: Made in USA* (2005, 2006), one of the 9/11 inquiry movement's leading lights, believes that George Bush didn't know in advance of the 9/11 terror attacks?

Tarpley also posits "a rogue network" operating above and beyond the White House dictating terror policy. In his newly published second edition of *Synthetic Terror* Tarpley writes:

> It was the rogue network that sent Bush an ultimatum on 9/11 with the words: "Angel is next," The meaning was: launch the war on civilization or be liquidated. Bush speedily complied, turning the U.S. government over to the rogue network." (p. 472)

Tarpley reiterated this theory in a talk he gave in NYC on January 15, 2006 (broadcast on NYC Community access cable on Jan. 24, 2006). Tarpley suggested that the reason that Bush was shunted from one military base to another before returning to Washington, D.C. on 9/11/01 was because he was threatened with execution if he didn't launch a war on civilization.

I suppose it all goes to show that everyone has his/her own individual understanding of the character of our leaders. We read into them our personal understanding of their temperament and personality and our own ideologies.

Nevertheless, I would have thought that Tarpley's fanciful idea of a rogue network dictating a war on civilization to Bush and threatening him with death was way too wacky for such a serious researcher.

For the record, there's no doubt in my mind that Bush himself was deeply involved in the planning and execution of the 9/11 terror events from the beginning. For one thing, there's plenty of mainstream documentation that the attack on Iraq was high on the agenda from the very minute that Bush took office in January 2001. Such an attack couldn't have taken place without 9/11. There's also indirect evidence that the attack on Iraq was planned at least as early as Bush was still a candidate for the Republican nomination for president in 2000.[53]

While I understand Bush to be ignorant, insensitive, narrow-minded, brutal, ruthless and sadistic, I don't believe he is stupid. In fact, I think he may even be intelligent (smart enough to get higher grades at Yale than Kerry).

I suspect that. like Reagan, he is an active participant in policy questions that interest him, while leaving the rest of the government to operatives like Karl Rove and Vice President Cheney.

Tarpley is one of the experts on the role of the secret government in creating policy and one might have expected from him a more sober look at their role. For example, in Carl Oglesby's brilliant *The Cowboy and Indian War* (1977) unfortunately out of print, the author presents evidence indicating that behind Eisenhower's back, Nixon conspired with the intelligence agencies to invade Cuba and remove Castro. According to Oglesby, Eisenhower later said he knew nothing about plans for an invasion of Cuba.

He thought that anti-Cuban preparations that were made during his administration were merely intended as guerrilla actions.[52] Oglesby points to one of the White House tapes where Nixon cryptically expressed concern about the possibility that his role in the invasion of Cuba might be exposed.

A nuanced view of the role of the secret government might suggest that their role varies from president to president. Had Nixon beat Kennedy in 1960, it seems a certainty that a full-scale U.S. invasion of Cuba would have followed. In the event, under Kennedy's leadership, the invasion turned into a fiasco, the CIA director Allen Dulles was fired, Kennedy was assassinated, and Allen Dulles was named to the Warren Commission which covered up the role of the secret government.

Many have pointed to the connection between the Kennedy assassination and 9/11. Tarpley himself makes this connection as does Joan Mellon, the author of *A Farewell to Justice: Jim Garrison, JFK's Assassination, and the Case That Should Have Changed History*.

In a talk she gave in NYC in late 2005 she expressly said that the lack of accountability for the JFK assassination paved the way for two generations of dirty tricks, false flags, etc., culminating in the 9/11 terror attacks.

It seems clear that some U.S. administrations, like Nixon's, Reagan's and George W. Bush's are much more in sympathy and work more closely with the secret government than do others. John F. Kennedy was the first and last president to openly wage war against them. □

9/11: REVELATIONS AND REFLECTIONS

by Nicholas Lysson

April 2007

Editor's Notes

Characteristic of many if not all false flags are the anomalies, the myriad inexplicable details which cry out for independent investigation. One of many such irregularities Nicholas Lysson cites is a statement made by NYC Mayor Rudy Giuliani where he lets slip his foreknowledge of the collapse of the North Tower. I couldn't help wondering if there was some connection between his evidently inadvertent public disclosure and the otherwise puzzling free fall collapse of his 2016 election campaign for president. Was it possible that questions and taunts from 9/11 "ravers" convinced him that if he continued his campaign, his complicity would be more widely exposed?

Meanwhile, Lysson's crystal clear prose is a marvel as he covers such stratagems as Operation Northwoods, Operation Gladio, the Lavon Affair; as well as such authors as Victor Ostrovsky, Daniel Glaser, Oded Yinon and more.

***

In February 2007 it came to light that on 9/11 both the BBC and CNN reported the fall of World Trade Center Building 7 well before it happened. The BBC was 23 minutes premature. Broadcast footage shows Jane Standley, the BBC correspondent, referring to the fall as a past event. At one point as she talks, the onscreen caption beneath the picture says the building "has also collapsed," in addition to the Twin Towers. But WTC 7 continues to stand, clearly visible. As she moves slightly, the building is mostly behind her left shoulder on the viewer's right. The live feed from New York breaks up before the actual collapse.

Aaron Brown on CNN announced that WTC 7 "has either collapsed or is collapsing" more than an hour before it fell. "We are getting information now," he says onscreen. Again, the standing building is clearly visible in the background. He turns around, sees it, and begins to backtrack.

Footage from these broadcasts has appeared on the Web. It has disappeared from some Web sites but seems now beyond effective recall. The counter on one of the remaining sites records over 300,000 visits, suggesting that the footage is in the hands of a great number of people who've downloaded it. A search on the combination of "BBC" and "9/11" and "WTC 7" quickly turns up copies. For CNN's coverage, substitute "CNN" for "BBC" in the same search combination.

An accurate prophecy of a skyscraper's collapse would be extraordinary. Apart from the three claimed instances on 9/11, no steel frame skyscraper has ever collapsed due to fire. On Feb. 13, 1975, the north WTC tower suffered a six-floor, three-hour fire with no suggestion of a collapse.

On Feb. 23, 1991, One Meridian Plaza, a 38-floor office building opposite Philadelphia City Hall, burned for 19 hours. An online analysis tells us that:

> Beams and girders sagged and twisted—some as much as three feet—under severe fire exposures, and fissures developed in the reinforced concrete floor assemblies in many places. Despite this extraordinary exposure, the columns continued to support their loads without obvious damage. (Emphasis added.)

One Meridian Plaza remained standing for another eight-and-a-half years, seemingly impossible to get rid of. Other examples of steel-frame indestructibility abound, such as the First Interstate Bank Building fire in Los Angeles on May 4, 1988.

WTC 7 was not hit by an airplane. Its collapse,[53] straight down and nearly at free-fall speed—neat as a top hat—was so mysterious as a matter of physics that the official 9/11 Commission report omits to mention it at all. On 9/11, Dan Rather, playing a videotape of the WTC 7 collapse, told the CBS audience it looked just like the controlled demolitions "we've all seen too much on television before," involving "well-placed dynamite to knock [a building] down." That part of Rather's broadcast, at least at this writing, is also available online.

The BBC has issued a response that doesn't deny the hysteron proteron [reversal of the natural order][54] in its coverage,[55] but doesn't explain it either:

> We're not part of a conspiracy. Nobody told us what to say or do on September 11th. We didn't get told in advance that buildings were going to fall down. We didn't receive press releases or scripts in advance of events happening.

The premature reporting from the BBC and CNN is reminiscent of Mayor Rudy Giuliani's admission on 9/11, to Peter Jennings of ABC News, that someone told him in advance that the WTC towers would fall:

> I went down to the scene and we set up headquarters at 75 Barkley Street, which was right there with the police commissioner, the fire commission-er, the head of emergency management, and we were operating out of there when we were told that the World Trade Center was going to collapse. And it did collapse...

Some have wondered who told Giuliani the buildings would collapse. The 9/11 Commission apparently never bothered to ask. Its report is silent on the point. See also Larry Silverstein's well-known account of the decision to "pull" WTC 7, on the PBS documentary "America Rebuilds," broadcast Sept. 14, 2002:

> I remember getting a call from the, er, fire department commander, telling me they were not sure they were gonna be able to contain the fire [in Building 7], and I said, "We've had such terrible loss of life, maybe the smartest thing to do is pull it." And they made the decision to pull and we watched the building collapse.

"Pulling" a building is jargon for controlled demolition. Silverstein was head of the group that entered into a 99-year lease for the WTC Twin Towers in the summer of 2001 and then greatly increased the insurance on the buildings. (Silverstein's group already controlled WTC 7.) Terrorist attacks were specifically covered under the augmented policies. The matter can be explored by searching on "Larry Silverstein insurance," which on Google brings up "about 202,000" items.

The BBC now says it no longer has its own archived footage from 9/11. It does not say who authorized this space-saving economy. That's led someone to post the official BBC News policy on creating and retaining archives. The policy requires that two broadcast-quality copies be preserved, plus one copy of "browser quality," to be used internally to spare the better copies. The policy does not state a time limit. On January 7, 2007, only a few weeks before the controversy erupted over its 9/11 footage, the BBC posted an online story that began:

> "BBC News opens archives to public...
> The fall of the Berlin Wall and footage of the 1966 England World Cup team are among items released from the BBC archives."

In other words, the footage is still available after 40 years, and probably a good deal longer. At least that's so with respect to particularly memorable events like a soccer championship in 1966. Who'd say 9/11 was less of a spectacle than that? Or of less importance than the fall of the Berlin Wall in 1989? And who'd care to bet the BBC has thrown out its coverage of the coronation of the present queen, all the way back in 1953?

But of course, 9/11 is different. That's why on Sept. 26, 2001, Giuliani banned picture taking at Ground Zero, and had the police confiscate film, and delete digital photographs from cameras. See http://911 research.wtc7.net/ wtc/groundzero/ restrictions.html.

Television footage was not the only new evidence that came to light in early 2007. See http://911research.wtc7.net/wtc/evidence/blueprints.html:

> The blueprints for the Twin Towers and Building 7 remained off-limits to the public for more than five years after the attack, despite the fact that the buildings were built with public money and that the engineering drawings of public buildings are supposed to be public information.

> In March of 2007 [however], an extensive set of detailed
> architectural drawings of the World Trade Center became public
> through the actions of a whistleblower [an event that went
> unmentioned in the mainstream media]. The 261 drawings
> included detailed plans for the North Tower . . . the World Trade
> Center foundation and basement, and the TV mast atop the North
> Tower. . . [S]ince the Twin Towers were of almost identical
> construction; it is safe to assume that the structural details that the
> drawings show for the North Tower are largely applicable to the
> South Tower.

The released drawings contradict the 9/11 Commission's statement that the core of each of the Twin Towers was merely "a hollow steel shaft." (See the fine print on p. 541, n. 1 of the commission's un-indexed report, claiming FEMA as the authority![56])

Rather, the drawings confirm what was already generally known, that each of the buildings was supported by 47 massive vertical steel box columns. Per the Web site just quoted:

> [T]he sixteen core columns that bounded the long faces of the
> buildings' cores had dimensions of 54 by 22 inches. The detailed
> drawings show that these columns maintained these dimensions
> through about the 66th floor.
>
> [Like steel columns in all tall buildings. . . the thickness of the
> steel in the core columns tapered from bottom to top. Near the
> bottom of the towers, the steel was four inches thick. . .

At the very bottom, the steel was five inches thick. Near the top, where the load was much less, the steel thinned to a quarter inch.

It would take near-simultaneous collapses of all 47 columns—at a cascading succession of identical levels—to bring either building straight down on its footprint.

The 9/11 Commission never explained how that might have happened, because it denied the very existence of the columns. But the collapses are all too readily explained in terms of controlled demolition. Dr. Steven E. Jones, a professor of physics at Brigham Young University, has posted several papers online suggesting that exactly this was done.

Jones says "the likelihood of near-symmetrical collapse of [WTC 7] due to fires (the 'government' theory) — requiring as it does near-simultaneous failure of many support columns — is infinitesimal. . . I conclude that the evidence for pre-positioned explosives in WTC 7 (also in towers 1 and 2) is truly compelling." Jones also says, "the observations of molten metal (I did not say molten steel!) in the basements of all three buildings, WTC 1, 2 and 7 [are] consistent with . . . the extremely high-temperature thermite reaction: iron oxide + aluminum powder – > Al_2O_3 + molten iron."

Since making those statements, Jones has posted a peer-reviewed paper at _http://www.physics. byu. edu/research/energy/ htm7.html_. Jones says in that paper that bringing a skyscraper down on its footprint is so difficult that only a handful of demolition companies in the world are willing to undertake it. He also says that Al Qaeda would have had no need of such precision because felling the buildings like trees, a much easier task, would have caused vastly more damage to lower Manhattan.

As a result of his outspokenness, Jones has been suspended from his teaching duties. [Editor's note: Prof Jones has since taken early retirement from BYU.]

The 9/11 story should also be considered in light of such false-flag schemes, American and Israeli, as Operation Northwoods and the Lavon Affair.

Operation Northwoods was a scheme, signed off on by every member of the Joint Chiefs of Staff in 1962, for terrorist activities in the United States that could falsely be attributed to Fidel Castro's Cuba, to justify a U.S. attack.

The Joint Chiefs even fantasized hopefully that the astronaut John Glenn might blow up on the launching pad, and that this could be attributed to Cuban electronic jamming. The plan was killed, either by the Pentagon's civilian leadership or by the Kennedy White House. See James Bamford, *Body of Secrets* (2001). The story was also picked up in *Harper's*, July 2001. The original JCS documents (15 pp.) can be found online.

The Lavon Affair involved an Israeli scheme, actually carried out, to have "Arab" terrorists bomb targets in Egypt that were associated with the U.S. and U.K. —libraries, theaters and the like. The conventional explanation is that Israel was trying to sabotage the relationship between the U.S. and the demonized Arab leader of the day, Gamal Abdel Nasser.

However, at pp. 107-14 of *Taking Sides: America's Secret Relations With a Militant Israel* (1989), Stephen Green adduces considerable evidence that the Lavon Affair involved a false false-flag operation, designed to go awry and be exposed as the work of the Israelis —and that the real target was not the relationship between Egypt and the U.S., but Israeli Prime Minister Moshe Sharett's efforts to negotiate a peace agreement with Egypt. Those efforts were indeed sabotaged, and by that measure, the apparent fiasco was a great success. On that telling, the plotters were militarists allied with David Ben Gurion and Moshe Dayan, and another of their concerns was sabotaging Agaf Modiin, the Israeli military intelligence organization, with which Mossad was contending for turf.

A great deal more along these lines can be found in Daniele Ganser, NATO's Secret Armies: Operation Gladio and Terrorism in Western Europe (2005). Operation Gladio was the subject of a series broadcast in England in 1992 by BBC2. The description of that series at Information Liberation.com is a good introduction:

> This BBC series [was] about. . . far-right secret arm[ies], operated by the CIA and MI6 through NATO, which killed hundreds of innocent Europeans and attempted to blame the deaths on Baader Meinhof, Red Brigades and other left-wing groups. Known as "stay-behinds," these armies were given access to military equipment which was supposed to be used for sabotage after a Soviet invasion. Instead, it was used in massacres across mainland Europe as part of a CIA "strategy of tension." Gladio killing sprees in Belgium and Italy were carried out for the purpose of frightening the national political classes into adopting U.S. policies.

That description of Gladio is prefaced with a lapidary epigraph from James Jesus Angleton, head of CIA counterintelligence, 1954-74: "Deception is a state of mind and the mind of the State."

Gladio was disclosed by Prime Minister Giulio Andreotti, in a speech to the Italian parliament on Aug. 3, 1991. For a variety of reasons, including Saddam Hussein's invasion of Kuwait the previous day, Andreotti's disclosure got little attention in the American media. Nor was there much attention when former Prime Minister Andreas Papandreou confirmed to the Greek daily Ta Nea that he had uncovered a similar structure in Greece. Nor was there much attention even when the German television channel RTL revealed that Gladio included former officers of Hitler's SS. See Secret Armies, pp. 1, 8, 15-16.

At p. 61, Ganser says that "due to his large experience in secret operations," President George H.W. Bush "was presumably well aware of the. . . terror the secret armies had been involved in."

At pp. 251-55 Ganser provides a partial summary of that terror, including the removal and hanging of Turkish Prime Minister Adnan Menderes; the false-flag kidnapping and murder of Italian Prime Minister Aldo Moro; other coups; the false-flag bombing of a waiting room in the Bologna train station, killing 85 and wounding over 200; and other massacres.[57]

According to the Mossad defector Victor Ostrovsky, The Other Side of Deception, p. 226 (1994), Mossad was one of the intelligence agencies involved with Gladio. In part that was through Licio Gelli. Now almost 90 and living under house arrest in his Tuscan villa, Gelli has had an interesting career. In his youth, he was a liaison officer between Mussolini's government and the Third Reich (and allegedly a Gestapo informant). He has often been identified as an organizer of the Bologna train station bombing. He has also been linked to Michael Ledeen of the Jewish Institute for National Security Affairs (JINSA). As to that organization, see Jason Vest, "The Men From JINSA and CSP," the Nation, Sept. 27, 2002. (CSP is the Center for Security Policy, which partially overlaps JINSA.) Ledeen is often identified as a source of the crudely forged documents that purported to show Iraq's recent quest for uranium in Niger.

Ostrovsky's story about Mossad, Gladio and Gelli concerns the early stages of what became the Iran-Contra affair, after the Iranian revolution of 1979 and Iraq's invasion of Iran in 1980. The story can be read to suggest that Ronald Reagan was telling the honest truth some years later when he told the American people he had no intention of trading arms for hostages. Reagan may have been focused instead on the main thrust of American and Israeli policy, which was to keep the Iran-Iraq war going as long as possible by selling arms to both sides. There were strategic benefits in keeping those countries embroiled with each other, and there was money to be made. The costs of the war, by some counts, including over a million Iraqi and Iranian lives, possibly as many as a million and a half, by the time it ended in 1988.

Secret Armies should be read together with Alfred W. McCoy's classic, The Politics of Heroin in Southeast Asia (1972). McCoy is a professor of history at the University of Wisconsin. He tells some of the other things the CIA did to curb leftist politics in Europe. For example, it permitted the "French Connection"—a plague on American blacks, just like the one on the "heathen Chinee" a century before—as a payoff to Corsican Mafiosi who beat up Communist organizers in Marseilles.

Compare Norman Lewis, Naples '44, pp. 120, 137-39 (1978) on how the U.S. handed over the civil administration of that city to Vito Genovese, an erstwhile capo di tutti capi in the American mob. Since 1937 Don Vito, as he liked to be called, had been visiting Italy because of a murder indictment in the U.S. While in Italy he first ingratiated himself with Mussolini, but then transferred his allegiance to the Allied Military Government. By the time he came home after his service, he was happy to have outlived all the witnesses against him.[58]

See also two books by Nafeez Mossaddeq Ahmed: The War on Truth: 9/11, Disinformation, and the Anatomy of Terrorism (2005), on the cultivation and sponsorship of militant Islamic terrorism by the intelligence services of the United States, Britain and Russia, beginning in 1979; and The War on Freedom: How and Why America was Attacked, September 11, 2001 (2002), which won the Naples Prize, Italy's most prestigious literary award, in 2003. Ahmed is a lecturer in international relations at the University of Sussex in England.

The 9/11 story should also be considered in light of the steadily growing list of admitted American "intelligence failures" about Iraq. Some of those intelligence failures concerning matters accurately predicted in Gen. H. Norman Schwarzkopf's memoir of the Gulf War of 1991, It Doesn't Take a Hero, p. 498 (1993): "From the brief time that we did spend occupying Iraqi territory after the war, I am certain that had we taken all of Iraq, we would have been like the dinosaur in the tar pit. ...."

The senior George Bush and his adviser Brent Scowcroft made the same point in A World Transformed, p. 489 (1998).

Other intelligence failures concerned matters examined and accurately reported by Ambassador Joseph Wilson and Hans Blix. Purportedly, the American intelligence community had no way of knowing what the invasion of Iraq would do to that nation's stability, or even what Saddam Hussein had been up to in the decade just past.

Of course, there's another way of looking at intelligence failures. See Ray McGovern, "Why Cheney Lost It When Joe Wilson Spoke Out," TruthOut.org, March 7, 2007. McGovern says that on the occasion of Wilson's famous op-ed piece for the New York Times:

> Adding insult to injury, Wilson chose to tell Washington Post reporters, also on July 6 [2003], in language that rarely escapes an ambassador's lips, the bogus report regarding Iraq obtaining uranium from Niger "begs the question regarding what else they are lying about."

That it does, which is the point of the present essay. On March 27, 2006, the New York Times reported an Oval Office meeting between George W. Bush and Tony Blair, held on Jan. 31, 2003, in which — according to a memorandum by David Manning, then Blair's chief foreign policy adviser — the two leaders acknowledged (to each other, not the public) that no weapons of mass destruction had been found in Iraq.[59] Manning's memorandum says "Mr. Bush [then] talked about several ways to provoke a confrontation, including a proposal to paint a United States surveillance plane in the colors of the United Nations in hopes of drawing fire. . . ." (Emphasis added.)

Such an operation would be a false flag in the literal sense. It would provide a fraudulent casus bello. Note who suggested it. Assess the character, stability and sagacity of that person. Consider motive, means and opportunity. Think, too, about the background from which George W. Bush emerged — possibly his main qualification in the eyes of the five Supreme Court justices who "elected" him.

For Bush, Operation Northwoods, Operation Gladio, the Lavon Affair and the like were all part of the culture, absorbed from childhood. That culture does not favor public candor. It favors manipulation, disinformation, and stampede.[60] Hence the famous smirk.

Why Would Anyone Suspect Israel of Complicity In 9/11?

In 1996, Richard Perle, David Wurmser, and Douglas Feith among others wrote a report for incoming Prime Minister Benjamin Netanyahu called "A Clean Break [from the Oslo peace process]: a New Strategy for Securing the Realm [Israel]." That report referred to "removing Saddam Hussein from power in Iraq [as] an important Israeli strategic objective in its own right," but primarily urged Saddam's removal as a means of putting pressure on Syria. Wurmser and Feith went on to hold high office in the George W. Bush administration, Wurmser as an adviser to Dick Cheney, Feith as the number-three man in the Pentagon, behind Donald Rumsfeld and Paul Wolfowitz…Perle became a high-level consultant to the Pentagon.

> As James Bamford points out in A Pretext for War (2004), the authors of "A Clean Break" urged a strategy that now looks suspiciously familiar. As Bamford describes it (pp. 262-63):
>
> As part of their "grand strategy," they recommended that Iraq [be] conquered and Saddam Hussein be overthrown [and] replaced by a puppet leader friendly to Israel. "Whoever inherits Iraq," they wrote, "dominates the entire Levant strategically." Then they suggested that Syria would be the next country to be invaded. "Israel can shape its strategic environment," they said. This would be done, they recommended to Netanyahu, "by reestablishing the principle of preemption," and by "rolling back" [Israel's] Arab neighbors. From then on, the principle
>
> would be to strike first and expand. . .They recommended launching a major unprovoked regional war in the Middle East. . . Then, to gain the support of the American government and public, a phony pretext would be used. . .

> . . . [A] way to win American support for a preemptive war
> against Syria, they suggested, was by "drawing attention to its
> weapons of mass destruction program."

The "Clean Break" strategy can actually be traced back a good deal further in Israeli planning. According to Oded Yinon, "A Strategy for Israel in the 1980s," *Kivunim*, a Journal for Judaism and Zionism (Dep't of Publicity, World Zionist Organization, Feb. 1982, available online):

> The dissolution of Syria and Iraq. . . into ethnically or religiously
> unique areas. . . is Israel's primary target on the Eastern front in
> the long run, while the dissolution of the military power of those
> states serves as the primary short-term target. Syria will fall
> apart, in accordance with its ethnic and religious structure, into
> several states. . . This. . .will be the guarantee for peace and
> security in the area in the long run, and that aim is already within
> our reach today.

Yinon had been a senior official of the Israeli Foreign Affairs Ministry. He became a journalist for the Jerusalem *Post.* Israel Shahak, who translated Yinon's article from the Hebrew, commented that:

> The idea that all the Arab states should be broken down by Israel into
> small units occurs again and again in Israeli strategic thinking. For
> example, Ze'ev Schiff, the military correspondent of Ha'aretz (and
> probably the most knowledgeable in Israel on this topic) writes about
> the "best" that can happen for Israeli interests in Iraq: "The
> dissolution of Iraq into a Shi'ite state, a Sunni state and the
> separation of the Kurdish part" (Ha'aretz 6/2[Feb. 6]/1982).

> *   *   *

> Actually, this aspect of the plan is very old. [The plan] follows
> faithfully the geopolitical ideas current in Germany of 1890-1933,
> which were swallowed whole by Hitler and the Nazi movement and
> determined their aims for East[ern] Europe. Those aims, especially
> the division of the existing states, were carried out in 1939-1941, and
> only an alliance on the global scale prevented their consolidation. . .

Those were indeed Nazi aims for Eastern Europe, especially for the Soviet Union and Poland. No copies of the *Generalplan Ost* survived the war (although it is referred to in other documents), but we have Heinrich Himmler's memorandum, *"Einige Gedanken über die Behandlung der Fremdvölkishen im Osten"* (May 5, 1940), stating a policy of fostering theretofore-nonexistent nationalities that would have mutually antagonistic separatist tendencies. Himmler's marginal notes say Hitler personally approved that policy.

Such a policy for the Middle East, with that provenance, might have been hard to sell by honest means to Americans. But there were other ways.

On August 14, 2006, Bill Christison—like Ray McGovern a veteran of long, high-level service in the CIA—published "Stop Belittling the Theories About September 11," at www. DissidentVoice.org. Christison says that:

After spending the better part of the last five years treating these theories with utmost skepticism, I have devoted serious time to actually studying them. . . I have come to believe that significant parts of the 9/11 theories are true and that therefore significant parts of the "official story" put out by the U.S. government and the 9/11 Commission are false.

http://patriotsquestion911.com/media.html (over 70 entertainment and media figures); *http://ae911truth.org/* (architects and engineers); *http://stj911.org/index.html* (Scholars for Truth and Justice);

http://physics911.net/ (physicists and other scientists); and *http://journalof911studies.org* (peer-reviewed papers on the collapse of the three WTC buildings).

He gives his reasons in detail. For similar conclusions of leading Republicans and military leaders (all but one retired from public life) see *http://georgewashington.blogspot.com/2007/03/911-and-right.html*, and the sites there are linked. See also such sites as *http://patriotsquestion911.com/professors.html* (some 130 professors); *http://patriotsquestion911.com/survivors.html* (over 100 survivors and family members);

Those are brave souls all. David Ray Griffin, a retired professor of the philosophy of religion, has written of how Bush took the official version of 9/11 to the level of religious myth (i.e., master societal narrative) by declaring war the next day from the pulpit of the National Cathedral. That myth draws its power from the primal American nightmare about have-nots and nonwhites. Hollywood has repeatedly sent Indiana Jones *with a bullwhip* to deal with Arabs. Would he carry that whip in Europe? Possibly in Muslim neighborhoods, he would.

Casting 9/11 as a religious myth means doubters can be punished as heretics—in some cases with loss of their jobs, word of which tends to travel—silenced, and held up to obloquy, all without the need of reasoned argument.[61]

One might respond: *E pur si muove.* Or repeat, with Daniel Defoe:

> Whenever God erects a house of prayer,
> The Devil always builds a chapel there.
> And 'twill be found, upon examination,
> The latter has the largest congregation.

NO PLANES ON 9/11 – EXPOSING THE ILLUSION

By Ronald Bleier

January 2007

"Irrefutable physics falsifies the Pentagon's lies."
-Morgan Reynolds

Editor's Notes

When I first learned of the brilliant work of Gerard Holmgren, uncovering the no planes, no Arabs, no hijackings version of what happened on 9/11, I had high hopes that his theory would achieve a consensus, at least within the 9/11 truth community. I was soon disabused. Holmgren was swiftly isolated, largely due, I gather, to the potent effectiveness of the plane meme and few learned that such a theory existed.

I found I had to wonder about my 9/11 truth colleagues who, it seemed, refused to examine or address no plane evidence whereas our mantra had been: Look at the evidence and decide for yourselves. So once again, I was taught the lesson that in politics, in religion and in other walks of life, we wear the suit that fits ourselves, not the suit that suits others.

In such cases, objective Truth takes a back seat to the subjective truth that emerges from the way our genes respond to our environment. It's the ideology the individual absorbs from her tribe and nation that determines belief, and we live and die with the truths that fit.

I'm reminded of the story of the aged Indian chief watching miles and miles of white settler wagon trains slowly moving into his territory. He smiles and says to his companion: "Now that they have all left the lands in the East, we can retake our former territory."

It'd be nice if the chief died not disillusioned.

***

L ike most people, on September 11ᵗʰ, 2001, I believed the official story about the terror attacks. It took me almost three years to become a skeptic. The major issue that led me finally to question the official accounts was the manner of the collapse of the Twin Towers. After watching a one-hour critical video in the summer of 2004 (see below) I decided to look into the question of whether the Twin Towers and Building 7 were brought down by pre-planned demolition charges. In due course, as I researched the issue in books, videos, and the internet, I become convinced that the terrible events of that day were planned and executed by the Bush administration. I saw no way out of Jim Hoffman's theory that if the WTC Towers were brought down by controlled demolition, then Osama Bin Laden couldn't have been responsible.[62]

Finally, to complete my conversion, about a year later, I read an article by Australian researcher Gerard Holmgren, called "Manufactured Terrorism,"[63] which propounded what seemed an incredible theory: that no large passenger jets were used in any of the 9/11 attacks, including New York City. Later I read yet another key article supporting the same No Planes Theory (NPT), this one by Morgan Reynolds,[64] former Chief Economist at the U.S. Department of Labor 2001-2002. I soon became an advocate of the NPT, a tiny subset of the 9/11-truth movement.

***

On the day of 9/11, I experienced a heavy dose of the intended shock and awe when I watched in real time the collapse of the Twin Towers. Shortly after 9:03 a.m. I heard on the radio that there was a video of a big passenger plane hitting the South Tower and I was glued to the TV for the next couple of hours.

Later I was relieved to learn that the government had quickly identified the perpetrators — the story was that they were Islamic extremists.[65] It wasn't much of a stretch for me to imagine that the motive for the attacks was revenge mainly for U.S./Israeli policies in the Middle East. The thought that my government, specifically the Bush-Cheney administration, might be the ones who planned and executed the attacks didn't enter my mind, nor would such an outrageous unthinkable idea seem to me for many months within the realm of possibility.

As I watched the World Trade Center towers collapse, I couldn't help thinking how surprising and fortunate it was that they came straight down in their own footprint instead of falling horizontally into the densely built-up neighborhood of lower Manhattan when the destruction in lives and property would have been vastly magnified.

Years later, I realized that that was a very vulnerable moment. All that it might have required for me to become an instant 9/11 skeptic was to learn that high-rise steel-framed buildings never come down at the speed of gravity and in their own footprints except during an earthquake or when previous arrangements have been made for them to collapse through controlled demolition. Dan Rather, CBS TV's venerable news anchor as he watched the collapse of WTC Building 7 at 5:20 p.m. said it was:

> "Reminiscent of those pictures we've all seen too much on television before when a building was destroyed by well-placed dynamite to knock it down."[66]

But I didn't happen to be watching television at that hour and in course of the day's traumatic events, I don't recall paying much attention to Building 7. I'm not sure that I even knew that Building 7 collapsed until I began my research in 2004.

The Strange Collapse of the Twin Towers

> There can't simultaneously be both **high resistance**—causing grinding of the concrete into dust—and **negligible resistance** allowing a fall at the same speed as through air. Only the input of extra energy—an orchestrated demolition, explains the simultaneous presence of both factors. – Gerard Holmgren (emphasis added)

It wasn't until the summer of 2004 that I saw a video of some of the speakers at a 9/11 conference held some weeks earlier in Canada. At that conference, persuasive evidence was presented that contradicted the official story, which claims that the towers collapsed as a result of the combination of plane crashes and the resultant fires.

One talk that I found most compelling was by computer engineer Jim Hoffman who has written widely on the World Trade Center collapses. From Hoffman and others, I learned that according to the laws of physics, even the combined impact of the "planes" and the resultant fires could not have caused the collapses and explosions.

The Strongest Smallest Fire in History

In Hoffman's presentation and in other videos, articles and books, it was pointed out that never before or since had steel-framed buildings been brought down by fire, even in cases where the fires were much hotter and burned much longer.

For example, the One Meridian Plaza fire in Philadelphia in 1991 burned for 18 hours and was described by local officials as the most significant fire in this century…The fire caused window breakage, cracking of granite, and failures of spandrel panel connections. Despite the severity and duration of the fire, as evidenced by the damage the building sustained, no part of the building collapsed… All other cases of large fires in steel-framed buildings were characterized by extensive window breakage, large areas of emergent flames and went on for several hours. The fires in the WTC towers did none of these things. [67]

David Ray Griffin, retired professor of Religion and Theology, a popular 9/11 author, writes that even a supporter of the official story, Thomas Eager, professor of materials engineering at MIT, says that the impact of the planes would NOT have been sufficient to bring down the Towers because "the number of columns lost on the initial impact was not large and the loads were shifted to the remaining columns in this highly redundant structure."[68]

I also learned that airplane fuel burns at only 800 degrees F, not nearly hot enough to seriously stress steel, which melts at 2700 F degrees in optimum conditions. Hoffman notes that steel is an excellent conductor of heat so that even if the steel beams in the immediate area of the crash were stressed, the heat would have been spread throughout the vast heat sink that comprised the 236 steel beams in the perimeter and the 47 steel beams built into the core of the building.

Thomas Eager asserts that the steel in the Towers could have collapsed if it had lost only 80% of its strength. Eager believes this happened since the fires reached 1300 F. But Griffin argues that for this amount of heat, the fires would have to be very big and it would have to be applied to a steel beam for a considerable amount of time.

(NPH, p. 14) The available evidence suggests that the fires were small and didn't burn for long. Griffin cites the photos in researcher Eric Hufschmid's book, Painful Questions[69] of the small fires evident in both Towers, which generated a great amount of heat but were not long-lasting because the fuel was quickly burned up.

Hufschmid's photos show that the spectacular flames vanished quickly and then the fire remained restricted to one area of the Tower and slowly diminished. The fires were localized and of short duration. (NPH, pp. 14-15) Griffin cites Hufschmid's question: How could a fire produce such incredible quantities of heat that it could destroy a steel building, while incapable of spreading beyond its initial starting location? The photos show that not even one floor in the South Tower was above the ignition temperature of plastic and paper!" The fire was not even powerful enough to crack glass windows! (NPH, p. 211, fn. 52)

Griffin tackles one of the persistent misunderstandings about the Twin Tower fires. He writes that defenders of the official theory suggest that the Twin Towers were special in the sense that the fire did not have to heat all the steel by spreading throughout the floors. The culprits were the "angle clips" which "held the floor joists between the columns on the perimeter wall and the core structure," and which, he says, were not designed to hold five times their normal load.

According to this "zipper" version of the truss theory, once angle clips failed in one area, it put extra load on other angle clips and then it unzipped around the building on that floor in a matter of seconds and led to a domino effect which caused the buildings to collapse within ten seconds. Something like this theory was endorsed in the FEMA report, which spoke of a "pancake-type of collapse of successive floors." (NPH, pp. 15-16)

But Griffin finds that there are problems with this account. First the amount of heat required to make the steel very hot would seem to require more heat than was present, especially in the South Tower.

2nd Griffin cites Hufschmid who writes, "In order for a floor to fall, hundreds of joints had to break almost simultaneously on 236 exterior columns and 47 core columns."

3rd Eagar's theory of the speed of the collapse – nearly at free fall speed--doesn't take into account the problem of resistance. "Can we really believe that the upper part of the buildings encountered virtually no resistance from the lower parts?" How "could the debris crush 100 steel and concrete floors while falling as fast as objects fall through air?"

4th Eager's and other versions of the official account cannot do justice to the total collapse of the towers, resulting in a pile that "was only a few stories high." Such theories don't explain the collapse of the steel core of the buildings.

5th The official story doesn't explain why the South Tower collapsed first. Since it would take considerable time for the fire to heat steel to its own temperature, all things equal, the South Tower, which was struck 17 minutes later than the North Tower, should have collapsed later, not 29 minutes earlier. This is even more surprising since the fires in the South Tower were much smaller. This "reversal of expectations suggests that the collapse of these buildings was caused by something other than the fires." (NPH, p. 17)

Controlled demolition accounts for all the facts discussed thus far. Peter Meyer, the author of a book on the WTC demolition, explained the reason the collapse was so total and so rapid. He theorized that the bases of the steel columns were shattered at the bedrock. "With those bases obliterated, and the supporting steel columns shattered by explosions at various levels...the upper floors lost all support and collapsed to ground level in about 10 seconds." (NPH, p. 18)

Griffin goes on to list additional facts that seem explainable only by the demolition theory.

Each collapse produced a lot of fine dust. Where does the energy come from to turn all this reinforced concrete into dust? Hufschmid adds that photos show only "a few small pieces of concrete" which means that virtually every piece of concrete "shattered into dust." Where did the energy come from? Similarly, by what means was very fine concrete dust ejected from the top of the building very early in the collapse. Hufschmid adds that even concrete slabs hitting the ground at free-fall speed would not be pulverized. That would require explosives. (NPH, p. 18)

Explosion Not Collapse

Evidence of the use of explosives can be seen in that the Towers didn't fall straight down, they exploded. Huge amounts of powder were "ejected horizontally from the building with such force that the buildings were surrounded by enormous dust clouds that were perhaps three times the width of the buildings themselves." Could any other power besides explosives turn concrete into powder and then eject it horizontally? And "some of the photographs show rather large pieces of the tower were thrown out 150 feet or more." (NPH, pp. 18-19)

Gerard Holmgren also points to the apparent floor-by-floor explosion (not collapse) of the Twin Towers and explains some of the physics involved. He finds that the conversion of the Towers into " a free falling collection of disconnected rubble," is possible only through "coordinated... demolition techniques." And:

> As if that isn't enough, we have the resistance paradox. This phrase has been coined to describe the fact that not only did the towers fall at a speed, which indicates negligible resistance, but at the same time they ground themselves into fine dust while still standing.

This is impossible under the law of conservation of energy. If one were to postulate that somehow the entire building was—without any planning—miraculously and symmetrically disembodied, enabling it to fall without resistance, then it leaves nothing to explain the pulverization of the concrete. Such pulverization can only come from a high-resistance collision. On the other hand, if you postulate extreme collision forces within the falling building, grinding the falling concrete into fine dust on its way down, then there is nothing to explain the resistance-free fall of the speed.

There can't simultaneously be both high resistance—causing grinding of the concrete into dust—and negligible resistance allowing a fall at the same speed as through the air. Only the input of extra energy—an orchestrated demolition, explains the simultaneous presence of both factors.[70]

The Pentagon Strike

Among the dozens of anomalies and unanswered questions pertaining to the attack on the Pentagon, researchers emphasize the difficulty in believing that no positive action was taken before 9:37 a.m. to protect the most well-guarded facility on the planet from an attack by a Boeing 757 passenger plane. Both Griffin and Holmgren point to the three different versions of the government's official story, none of which explained why there were no timely interceptions of the four alleged passenger jets.[71] The official story might have gained far less currency if, for example, the media had informed the public that military jet interceptions of wayward aircraft are routine and occur more than a hundred times a year. [77]

Morgan Reynolds finds a "gaping hole in the government theory" of how the Pentagon was struck by a Boeing 757 and he reproduces a helpful diagram.

Reynolds finds that the Pentagon gash is too small both vertically and horizontally. A Boeing 757's tail is 40 feet tall with landing gear up while the maximum height of the hole in the Pentagon could not have been 30 feet tall (two stories).

The width of the hole was less than 20 feet before the façade collapsed, and windows above the impact hole were intact. The largest width claimed for the hole is 65 feet—more like 52 feet according to photographic expert Jack White—and that was after the façade collapsed, not upon impact. The 757 wingspan is 125 feet, about twice the width of the post-façade-collapse hole. The Puny Pentagon Hole (PPH) falsifies the government's "a-Boeing-757-hit-the-Pentagon" story. It is not a close call.

Reynolds also points to some of the impossible physics that would have had to transpire had flight AA77 struck the Pentagon in accord with the official story. Simply put, no passenger jet could have flown at ground level at top speed because the resultant air pressure acting on the wings would have thrown the plane wildly off course even with the most experienced of pilots.

> A 757 flying a nearly flat flight profile (no dive) at 500+ mph as alleged could not hit the Pentagon's ground floor because of an extremely powerful ground effect cushion beneath it. At high speeds, the highly energized wing-tip vortices and huge downwash sheet of a 200,000-lb. airliner makes it physically impossible to get closer to the ground than one-half wingspan or about 60' in this case. The physical forces of the compressible gas called air, in other words, stirred by a high-speed 757 traveling flat near the ground make it impossible to land it at high speed. An aeronautical engineer proves this proposition in an *article* at *www.physics911.net*, and he invites other engineers and pilots to prove him wrong. Very few pilots have experienced the aerodynamic effects in this rare flight domain because they normally only get this close to the ground during landing at low speeds. Highly wing-loaded aircraft like the Global Hawk or B1-B can land at high speed but not lightly

wing-loaded aircraft like the 757. In addition, a ground-hugging 757 spewing a 100,000-lb. thrust jet blast behind it would have blown trailer trucks and people away, phenomena absent in the flight path (see the DVD "*Loose Change*" for an example). Irrefutable physics falsifies the Pentagon's lies.

No Planes in D.C. or in PA?!

There are so many unanswered questions related to the alleged crash of a Boeing 757 flying into the Pentagon that perhaps a majority of the 9/11 research community don't believe that a Big Boeing was involved in that attack. Many skeptics also don't believe there is any evidence of a passenger jet plane at the alleged crash site in Shanksville, PA.[72] Thus for the NPT to be more favorably viewed by the 9/11 research community it remains only to rule out that passenger jets were used to crash into the Twin Towers. Morgan Reynolds helpfully sets the stage.

> The one towering fact is that the 9-11 research community can prove beyond a reasonable doubt that professional demolition brought down the three trade center buildings—WTC 1, WTC 2 and WTC 7. These unprecedented collapses in steel-framed skyscrapers bear all the earmarks of demolition—virtual free fall speed of collapse, pulverization of concrete, eyewitness testimony of explosions, film, and photographic evidence of explosions, and so on. The jetliner attacks, by contrast, might be described as diversions that facilitated and covered the primary attacks via demolition, a familiar tactic in terrorist attacks.[73]

Morgan Reynolds argues that it is important to address the No Planes Theory despite objections by many, evidently the majority of the 9/11-Truth movement, that such questions will prove a "sideshow" or a "distraction" from "an uncompromising focus on the WTC demolitions."

Reynolds reminds us that the official story that "young Arabs hijacked specific flights and crashed them is a vital component of the official fiction."

> A new, rational understanding about the plane stories would have great value, and that probably explains the intense resistance to

such scrutiny. Questions and answers about each plane crash matter for at least three reasons:

* If the perpetrators get away with the plane hoaxes, it encourages more audacious, blood-soaked scams.
* The key to acquiescence in the government's war on terror and global domination project is public belief in Arab hijacked airliners and crashes.
* Exposure of airplane lies expands the proof that the government committed the 9/11 atrocities.[79]

Gerard Holmgren: No Planes, No Hijackers

In order to provide meaningful context to his discussion of problems with the official story about 19 Arab hijackers, Holmgren discusses the inexplicable movements and the apparent inaction and disinterest of President Bush and Acting Chairman of the Joint Chiefs of Staff, General Richard Myers, during the attacks; the almost instant naming of Osama bin Laden as the culprit despite claims by the U.S. that they were taken completely by surprise.

The immediate threat to invade Afghanistan when it turned out the decision to do so had already been made by July 2001 and the plans were on Bush's desk by Sept 9; and the urban myth that Bin Laden claimed responsibility for the attacks.[74]

Among other things, Holmgren wonders how credible it can be that the FBI so quickly identified 19 Arab hijackers within only a few days. He also cites their difficult-to-believe allegation that some of the hijackers' passports and suicide notes were found at the crash scenes. "In another miraculous stroke of good luck," Holmgren writes, "the luggage of the supposed ringleader, Mohammad Atta, was "fortuitously left behind at Logan airport" with instructions to his fellow conspirators.

Holmgren opines that it must have been embarrassing for the FBI when some of the hijackers began turning up alive and protesting their innocence. "And even more embarrassing when the passenger lists provided by the airlines did not contain a single Arabic name," and he details other related impossibilities, improbabilities and coincidences, including an admission by the FBI (later apparently effectively recanted) that "they actually had no idea who hijackers were." To this day, the FBI list of the 19 hijackers remains unchanged.[75]

Among the reasons that Holmgren concludes that there weren't any hijackings or hijackers was that in not one of the four alleged hijackings did any of the crew punch in the four-digit hijacking code to alert Air Traffic Control.

Holmgren also wonders why there was no distress call from Flight AA 11 (North Tower hit) when there was an alleged 25-minute standoff, including shooting and stabbing of passengers. Another anomaly from that alleged flight is that "the timeline of the alleged phone call indicates that the plane had already turned off course before the hijackers got into the cockpit."

No Verifiable Wreckage at the Pentagon

Holmgren continues his line of argument by claiming that the plane that we saw on TV was "an elaborate illusion." Holmgren begins his analysis of the planes with AA77, the plane supposedly involved in the Pentagon attack.

He suggests that the reason that the government has not produced clear and undisputable video evidence of a big passenger plane striking the Pentagon *is because it never happened.*[76]

From photos of the aftermath, he can find no evidence of wreckage of such a plane: "no wings, no tail, no protruding fuselage." Holmgren also reminds us that early reports on 9/11/01 said that a truck bomb caused the damage to the Pentagon. The "witness reports are confused and contradictory and provide no confirmation of a large plane hitting the building." [77] (Holmgren's emphasis)

BTS Data Reveal No Passenger Planes Destroyed On 9/11

If the subject were not so controversial, one might assume that a very powerful blow to the story of four hijacked airplanes on 9/11 would be Holmgren's discovery that two of the four flights connected to that day's events did not exist and the other two alleged participating aircraft were not destroyed until four years later.

As Holmgren writes, the Bureau of Transportation Statistics (BTS) keeps detailed records of flight times, tail numbers, taxi out times, wheels-off times, and so on for every scheduled flight from a U.S. airport, in part for liability insurance considerations. Holmgren found that the original BTS records of take-offs that day did not list flights for AA77 (Pentagon crash) and AA11 (North Tower, the first hit).[78]

Of the first hit on the WTC North Tower at 8:46, Holmgren notes that when one looks closely at the video (which wasn't broadcast until 16 hours later "when the official story of four large planes had already been put into the public's mind") all one can see is "a brief flash and then the explosion." Holmgren claims that whatever the object is, it "is certainly not a Boeing 767 or any kind of large passenger jet." The object is "way too small. It dive bombs into the tower in a manner which would appear to [be] impossible for a large airliner."

Although, he writes, "the natural tendency is to think it is just too fast to see on the video…a frame by frame enlarged analysis…shows a very strange looking object, or possibly several objects flying in close formation. A pulsating blob or group of blobs is probably the best description." [79]

Holmgren argues that the passenger lists seem to be fabricated "because there are impossible contradictions between the lists published by different media outlets…." Nor, he claims, are there any reliable witnesses to support a large jet of the first strike. "All early reports say that it was a small plane or missile," and others say they simply didn't see any plane.

According to Holmgren, the first strike became a "large plane after people saw the second strike live on TV, leading to the assumption that the first strike had been the same thing," and after American Airlines declared that it had lost AA11 in the crash.

The Illusion -- Live on TV?!

Holmgren then deconstructs "the South Tower strike – the second hit, the one shown live on TV" and acknowledges that superficially it certainly appears to be a large jet." Yet, he argues, "a close examination reveals that it is not a real plane." To support this assertion Holmgren provides a score of links to the work of researchers Rosalee Grable (aka Web Fairy), Nico Haupt, Morgan Reynolds, Ivan Amato[80] and his own supporting articles.[81]

Holmgren finds that the plane shown on TV is not real because it "shows impossible physical characteristics and behavior." The argument that I find most convincing and easiest to understand is his claim that one can see in a frame-by-frame analysis that the alleged plane "passes through the wall like a ghost without making a hole and without breaking off any parts." Holmgren concludes that the plane is "simply a cartoon, which has been animated into the footage."[82]

According to Holmgren, despite popular misconceptions that many real-time videos of the plane striking the South Tower exist, there was only one live video of this plane and that video did not show it hitting the building, but rather it shows the plane passing behind the building "giving the impression that it impacted the hidden face," an effect easily achieved "with commercially available real-time animation technology. The other videos, which seem… to show the plane actually hitting the building did not appear until hours later.

Holmgren makes short work of flight UA 93, the one alleged to have crashed in Shanksville, PA. This was also "a bona fide flight, but the plane −N591UA − was also still registered as valid for more than four years after Sept 11…The alleged crash site in Pennsylvania shows absolutely no evidence of a plane crash."

To drive home his point that no planes were involved in the 9/11 attacks, Holmgren makes much of the lack of evidence of any wreckage of any of the four planes. He suggests that if real planes had crashed, it would be an easy matter for the government to produce some portion of the tons of normally identifiable wreckage.

Likewise, Morgan Reynolds finds that the most obvious defect of the official story is the absence or near absence of conventional airplane wreckage.

> The government could have ended the controversy over planes
> long ago by allowing independent investigators to examine part
> numbers and compare them to each plane's maintenance
> logbook. This did not happen following the 9/11 crashes. The

government has not produced a single airplane part by serial number for independent corroboration. (My emphasis)

Of the two Boeing 767's, which vanished into the Twin Towers, Reynolds asks:

How could two large wide-bodied aluminum jetliners penetrate massive steel towers and disappear with no deceleration visible, no plane wreckage visible in gashes and none knocked to the ground below the impact zone?

Reynolds finds a "stunning lack of evidence" that "no confirmed debris exists from two alleged 767 high speed crashes into skyscrapers within 17 minutes of each other. Furthermore, Reynolds finds that:

Physics rejects any theory that posits an invincible airplane (a plane remaining intact after an abrupt collision with a steel skyscraper) that also disintegrates (flimsy) in the next instant in the same general physical environment (temperature, etc.)…(My emphasis)

Another problem, says Reynolds, is that the maximum spread across the north tower hole is 126 feet and the south tower is only 103 feet, opening insufficient to accommodate a 767 wingspan of 156 feet." "Wings with momentum do not "fold back onto themselves" in order to slip through an undersized hole along with the fuselage." Summing up this line of argument, Reynolds writes:

Defenders of the 767 theory want their cake and eat it too: supposedly powerful 767s easily penetrated steel walls and floors yet identically crumbled within a fraction of a second and vanished inside despite huge fuselage length and wingspan ¾ the length of a tower wall. Both 767s were never seen again from any side of either tower, a dazzling combination of imposing strength and fragility within a tenth of a second. (My emphasis)

Holmgren – Why They Didn't Use Planes

In his article on "Why they didn't use planes," Holmgren suggests that barring an independent investigation, it is impossible to do justice to the question.

Yet he thinks it may be instructive to outline some of the thinking that could have gone into planning the operation. In Holmgren's view, the perpetrators had to weigh the dangers inherent in their two main options: either use real passenger planes or use missiles (or some other similar method or combination of methods of creating an explosion) and convince people that the missiles were planes.

In the missile-not-planes scenario, Holmgren suggests that there are two things that could go wrong. The first is that witnesses would say (as they did in reality) that they didn't see a plane involved in the first strike. Holmgren suggests that this problem was easily countered in part because there was only an 18-minute window between the first hit at 8:46 and the second at 9:03 when everyone saw "a big jet live on TV." Those witnesses who said they didn't see a plane strike the North Tower were effectively intimidated or ignored.

According to Holmgren, in the brief period between the two strikes, there was only one witness who said he saw a large jet strike the North Tower, "and that just happened to be the vice prez of CNN…" Thus the problem of "contrary witnesses [turned out to be] a minor inconvenience…easily overcome with good planning."
The second problem the planners of 911 probably foresaw is that there would be some who would look at the tapes and discover that the video of the second hit was a cartoon. But Holmgren believes they figured that such contrary information would be minimized by the shock and awe of the occasion and the onslaught of their propaganda campaign. Writing in 2005, Holmgren concludes, that despite grumbling from a few researchers and critics like Rosemary Grable (a/k/a Web Fairy)[83] their choice of strategy not to use planes worked out successfully as they had planned. [91]

Problems With Using Real Planes

Holmgren develops his discussion of the problems with using real jets with the two choices of piloting them with suicide pilots or piloting the jets by remote control.

Some of the "obvious...and monstrous difficulties" of using real pilots are not difficult to imagine. What if, for example, the Arab pilots haven't been trained to fly jets?

Or if they haven't been trained to fly jets without responding to ground control? What if they don't wake up in time to make their flights? Eric Hufschmid, an advocate of the theory that the passenger jets were piloted by remote control, asks similar questions: "What if the hijackers decide to switch from hitting the World Trade Center to hitting the U.S. Capitol...or they miss the towers and hit some other building?"[84]

Holmgren takes up the many problems with the remote-control theory. This theory splits into the two options of "crashing a plane with passengers aboard or with no passengers aboard." According to Holmgren, both "possibilities create potentially insurmountable problems with the cover-up."

A remotely controlled plane might "hit some other building, just clip its wing on the tower and crash into the streets or cause a cascade of damage on other non-targeted buildings, miss altogether and finish up in the Hudson..."

Holmgren suggests that "Even the smallest increase in the risk of the target not being hit properly would be completely unacceptable, given the easily manageable nature of any problems associated with the alternative [missile] scenario." According to Holmgren, "missing the target is only the beginning...What about the aftermath?"

For example, an unacceptable outcome would be if the plane missed or slightly missed its target and it was found that there were no passengers. Similarly, if there were passengers and one or more survived to tell their story.

Even if no passengers survived, innocent rescue workers might arrive before the cover-up crew and discover and release forensic evidence inimical to the cover story.

Any of these outcomes would be "Far worse than anything a few witnesses could say in the 18 minutes between the two tower strikes…. In addition, real planes leave real wreckage… which means real flight recorder boxes to be found and more stuff to hush up…"

Holmgren concludes with some of the commonsense notions familiar to veterans of TV police procedurals.

> In committing a crime, the idea is to leave as little mess as possible, because every bit of mess is a potential clue. Even in the event of a successfully
> targeted crash, real aircraft, scattering wreckage and bodies everywhere creates an enormous amount of mess to cover up compared to the relatively neat problem of a few witnesses and a few conspiracy nuts trying to tell people what the video shows.
>
> The problems of the real plane scenario are enormously compounded by the possibility of a botched crash, which itself is a significantly increased risk when using big lumbering jets not specifically designed for that task as opposed to precision weaponry which is far more reliable.

Not Many Plane Crash Victims

A frequently asked and presently unanswerable question is: what happened to the passengers and crew of the four passenger jets that were supposed to have crashed? While very little information about their deaths has surfaced there is evidence that there were fewer victims than has been reported.

NY-based researcher Vincent Sammartino claims that the government seems to have faked the number of plane victims and also faked the number who claimed victim compensation.[85]

According to Sammartino, of the 266[86] official names of passengers and crew who were supposed to have died in the four passenger jets, only 52 names have appeared on the Social Security Death Index (SSDI), a privately owned website not affiliated with the Social Security Administration. According to Sammartino, of the 52 listed as dead in the SSDI, which has an accuracy rate of about 83%, only 11 of the family members have claimed victim compensation (not counting 9/11 plane crash widow, Ellen Mariani, who has pointedly refused compensation).

Sammartino writes that his research was spurred in part because of a radio interview he heard with Ms. Mariani and her lawyer in which they spoke of their inability to locate other family members of the purported plane passengers.

If Sammartino's figures are closer to reality than official reports, the discrepancies also go some way to advancing the NPT. If no planes were involved in the 9/11 attacks, and if Holmgren is right that Flights 11 and 77 did not fly that day (and Flights 93 and 175 did not crash that day), then it might have been easier for the terrorists to have diverted and perhaps disposed of merely 60-70 victims rather than many more bodies.

Thus the NPT helps us to advance, as Holmgren suggests, a combination of missile, and preplanned explosives theory to explain the explosions and fires at the Twin Towers and the Pentagon and the lack of any big passenger plane evidence at those sites. It also helps to explain why relatively few "plane crash" victims have come forward. Evidence also indicates that no big passenger plane (or any other plane) crashed in Shanksville, PA. The episode may have been cooked up simply for purposes of distraction.

Occam's Razor

[If the Towers were brought down by controlled demolition,] "why bother with the planes at all?"

As an independent researcher with little at stake in any particular theory, it has been relatively easy for me to follow the NPT evidence where it leads. I have joined the No Planes group in part because it seems to me most in conformity with Occam's Razor, the least complex theory that accounts for the available data.

Over and above scores of non-passenger plane related 9/11 anomalies, the NPT seems to provide a common-sense explanation for many of the unanswered questions and inconsistencies. For example, the NPT explains:

a) why government BTS records show that two of the four planes never took off that day and two others were not decommissioned until four years later.

b) why the government has refused (or been unable) to present "a single airplane part by serial number for independent corroboration," and why there is no confirmed debris of any of the alleged four planes so that all of them have disappeared without a trace.

c) why the passenger lists are phony; why no Arabic names are on any of the authenticated passenger lists; and why there are remarkably few alleged plane victims' families requesting compensation

d) why several of the purported hijackers have turned up alive and why the government apparently felt it necessary to produce such unpersuasive evidence as hijacker passports, training manuals, etc.

e) why in the immediate aftermath of the attacks, the government claimed that there were terror cells operating in at least 40 states but hasn't produced even one untainted terror cell in the last five years.

f) why there is no reliable video of the Pentagon and the NYC Twin Tower attacks? In the case of the Pentagon video released by the government first as photo stills and then as video, no plane is in evidence; nor would it be possible for a big passenger jet to come in at ground level at high speed.

g) why there was no air cover in NYC or in Washington, D.C. until after the Pentagon attack at 9:37. If there were no hijacked planes there would have been no need for interceptions.

h) why there are no credible witnesses to ANY of the alleged four planes?

i) why the authorities destroyed the tapes of the flight controllers' recollections of the events of that day? Those tapes might contain evidence that flights 11 and 77 did not take off that day and that 175 and 93 did not crash.

j) why ALL the cell phone calls were fabricated including the iconic "Let's Roll," call as well as the Ted Olson-Barbara Olson exchange. [87]

Arab Extremists – A Comfortable Image

One reason for the success of the official story seems to be that many are comfortable with the meme[88] that Osama Bin Laden and 19 Islamic extremists were responsible for the terror on 9/11.

The cultural and political tropes induced by the half-century-long Israeli-Palestinian conflict and the wider Arab-Israeli conflict have conditioned many in the West to accept the notion of Muslim fanatics willing and capable of suicide attacks on the U.S. homeland. Pro-Israeli sentiment reaches deep into the grassroots which is constantly fortified by powerful public relations campaigns of pro-Zionist pressure groups and their academic, political and media supporters. In addition, upon the demise of the Soviet Union, the U.S. substituted Islamic terrorism as a means of justifying and enlarging the national security state a la Orwell. Thus, a perfect storm of dominant forces continues to impose the notion of Muslim responsibility for 9/11 terror. Once the government identified the perpetrators on the morning of 9/11,[89] it became an uphill task to convince people to take contrary evidence seriously.

Much of the reluctance to give up on the notion of Muslim terrorists also seems to pervade elements of the 9/11 research community. Despite the lack of any independently verifiable evidence of Arab suicide bombers, many appear to prefer to hold onto this meme perhaps because they also find at least a grain of truth in the stereotype of Islamic fanatics.

But perhaps an even stronger motive for insisting on planes in NYC lies in the fear of many 9/11 skeptics that the image of a plane crashing into the South Tower is so convincing that advocating the NPT would bring discredit on the 911 Truth community. As Professor James Fetzer, a well-known 9/11 activist has put it: Even if they (the advocates of NPT) are right, "it hurts the movement." Many feel that there is so much evidence of government complicity beyond the issue of big passenger jets that diverting attention to the one thing most people believe that they "saw" is not to our tactical and strategic advantage.

Yet, in one sense the battle has already been won: the inconsistencies and absurdities of the official story are such that a July 2006 poll by Scripps News Service indicated that 36% of Americans -– about 72 million people -– suspect that federal officials assisted in the 9/11 attacks or took no action to stop them.[90] Doubtless, as time goes on, more will gather to the cause as they learn of contrary evidence. But to translate these millions of people into effective political action that would dramatically revise the official story would require a revolution in political awareness – one that hasn't yet happened, for example, with regard to the assassinations four decades ago of JFK, MLK, and RFK. Revolutions sometimes happen but they tend to be rare because they require a confluence of difficult-to-manufacture elements including inspired leadership, and extraordinary outside circumstances.

It's hard to imagine the kind of revolution that would be necessary to pry open the files and reveal the "deep politics," the secret government, and their black operations and their false flags that are the staple of elements of the security and intelligence services. Elements of the CIA, the FBI, the NSA, and military intelligence have worked more or less closely with the various post-WWII U.S. administrations. On one extreme would be the case of JFK, who seems to have been assassinated by them in part because they couldn't abide his politics. The others have been the Reagan, Bush I and II administrations, which work closely with them.

Meanwhile, it may be better to view the struggle for justice as a long-term one and coalesce on a strategy that places the evidence first and foremost. As Gerard Holmgren has emphasized, the 9/11-Truth movement should stand for truth above all. One notable advantage of concentrating on the evidence is that it will distinguish us from ideologues of all stripes. It's also a comfort in a whirlwind to reflect that in the long run truth can sometimes be the strongest weapon.

Bush, Cheney, Rumsfeld – Radical Extremists

> *Our enemies are innovative and resourceful, and so are we. They never stop thinking about new ways to harm our country and our people, and neither do we.*

> - President George W. Bush (2004)

Few in the 9/11-Truth community doubt that the motive for the attacks was the Bush administration's determination to create the pretext for the wars against Afghanistan and Iraq and going forward perhaps new wars in 2007 against Syria and Iran.
Many have pointed to the neoconservative Project for the New American Century document, "Rebuilding America's Defenses," written or subscribed to by such figures as Dick Cheney, Donald Rumsfeld and Paul Wolfowitz which outlined plans for an "aggressive imperialism" that could not be accomplished without the new Pearl Harbor that 9/11 provided.[91]

The 9/11 hoax in conjunction with the September 2001 anthrax attacks on Democratic Senators Daschle and Leahy enabled a bogus "war on terrorism," and an extremist attack on our constitution and civil liberties.

The administration's successfully completed agenda has so far included the Patriot Act, the rollback of habeas corpus, mass warrantless wiretapping and probable data mining, the routine torture of prisoners, hundreds of millions of dollars in contracts to build "temporary detention facilities," the "unitary" presidency and much more.

In addition, 9/11 gave the Bush administration a raison d'etre and a legitimacy hitherto lacking. Before the September 2001 attacks, polls reflected widespread public disapproval of the new Bush administration in part because it was evident that they lacked a positive national or international agenda.

They seemed bent on removing the government from any constructive role in the civic life of the country. They openly pushed for the removal of environmental and regulatory safeguards; they prized power over diplomacy, and they plunged this country into reckless and unsustainable budget-busting fiscal and tax policies.

Year Zero

Activist and author Naomi Klein traveled to Baghdad in 2004 and published an article entitled "Baghdad Year Zero."[92]
As her subtitle, "Pillaging Iraq in pursuit of a neocon utopia," suggests, she attributes to one faction in the Bush administration the belief that "Iraq was so contaminated that it needed to be rubbed out and remade from scratch." She reports that she saw much rubbing out but little if any remaking.

Bush administration's talk of bringing democracy to the Middle East fooled few although it served at the time and seems still to work well for many "talking heads." The purpose of the invasion of Iraq was to destroy the country.

The destruction of Iraq would also cohere with the fanatical pro-Israeli proclivities of the neocons who seek to ensure that a nationalist Iraqi challenge to Israeli domination of the Middle East will never be possible. Zionist interest in maintaining the U.S. occupation of Iraq goes a long way toward explaining why the Democrats in particular are effectively giving carte blanche to Bush's plans for an indefinite U.S. occupation.

In addition, the consequences of Bush administration policies are likely to bring on Year Zero to the United States and the rest of the world as well. They seem determined to remove the possibility of a positive role for government everywhere.

In the classic film "It's a Wonderful Life," the James Stewart character is presented with a nightmare vision of what life in his town would have been like absent his beneficent work. Our current all-too-real nightmares, the ones ongoing in so many countries -- Afghanistan, Iraq, Darfur, Burma, Palestine, Zimbabwe, North Korea, Somalia, the underside of America, and elsewhere, are tragic testimonies to the power of ruthless people in high places bent on permanent war and destruction for its own sake. □

PRE- AND POST-9/11 FALSE FLAGS - HOW WEAPONS OF MASS DECEPTION ARE INTERDEPENDENT

By Kevin Barrett

Dr. Barrett offered the following bio:

Kevin Barrett, Ph.D., an American Muslim and Islamic Studies scholar is one of America's best-known critics of the War on Terror.

A specialist in North African Studies and Sufism, his career underwent a sudden shift in 2006, when Wisconsin state legislator Steve Nass and 60 Republican colleagues demanded he be fired from his teaching position at the University of Wisconsin-Madison due to remarks he made on Jessica McBride's WTMJ radio show characterizing 9/11 as a false flag operation. Although UW-Madison initially refused to fire him and his students gave him high marks, the witch-hunt created an un-erasable Internet "paper trail" that left him "politically unemployable," as whistleblowers on two hiring committees, including Dr. Howard Ross at U.W.-Whitewater, have observed.

Since then Dr. Barrett has authored and edited several books, including Truth Jihad (2007), 9/11 and American Empire, Vol. 2 (2007), Questioning the War on Terror (2008), We Are NOT Charlie Hebdo (2015), ANOTHER French False Flag (2016) and Orlando False Flag (2016). He has edited and translated From Yahweh to Zion by Laurent Guyenot (2018). Dr. Barrett has appeared many times on Fox, CNN, PBS and other broadcast outlets.

He has inspired feature stories and op-eds in The New York Times, The Christian Science Monitor, the Chicago Tribune, and other mainstream publications. He also authored the first three mainstream American newspaper op-eds (in The Capital Times of Madison, Wisconsin) calling 9/11 an inside job, and organized Dr. David Ray Griffin's April 2005 talk at UW-Madison nationally telecast on C-SPAN. A former teacher at colleges and universities in Paris, the San Francisco Bay Area, and Wisconsin, Dr. Barrett currently works as author, talk radio host, False Flag Weekly News host, editor at Veterans Today, and international TV pundit. His website is TruthJihad.com.

***

Editor's Notes

Aside from the high-profile false flags of 9/11 and the JFK assassination, there are many others that Dr. Barrett contextualizes and deconstructs. A portrait emerges of how the government routinely uses and rationalizes terror to enforce public acceptance of its permanent war agenda. Its internal catchphrase is: The enemy must be created and sustained.

(The following is an excerpt from We Are NOT Charlie Hebdo! Free Thinkers Question the French 9/11 (2015)

W

e interpret new information by comparing it to past experiences—more precisely, to stories we tell ourselves about past experiences. If we have perceived an apparent pattern, such as angry Muslims reacting violently when their Prophet is insulted, we assume that each new incident, such as the Charlie Hebdo attack, must fit the same template. It is these "public myths," as they are called by self-styled public mythmaker Philip Zelikow, that structure the social reality we inhabit. And as Zelikow notes, it doesn't matter whether or not they are true; the important thing is that they are widely believed to be true.

One of the public myths that grounds Americans' and Europeans' understanding of their political systems is the myth of the lone nut. Assassinations of powerful and influential individuals, public outbursts of violence with political consequences—these are generally attributed to marginalized individuals or groups, rather than to the powerful individuals and institutions that stand to benefit from the crimes. Each new incident, each new lone nut, each new terrorist attack, is written off in advance as another example of senseless violence, of the lashing out of the marginalized.

But what if there are other patterns at play? What if such violence is more often instrumentalized than random? What if much of the spectacular mayhem fed to us by the media has been fabricated by those who gain from it?

Lance deHaven-Smith writes in his groundbreaking *Conspiracy Theory in America*:

> The tendency to consider suspicious political events individually and in isolation rather than collectively and comparatively is not limited to the conspiracy-theory literature; it is built into the conspiracy-theory label and has become a pervasive predisposition in U.S. civic culture. For Americans, each assassination, each election breakdown, each defense failure, and each war justified by "mistaken" claims is perceived as a unique event arising from its own special circumstances. While Americans in the present generation have personally witnessed many political crimes and tragedies, we see them as if through a fly's eye, situating each event in a separate compartment of memories and context.[93]

Smith asserts that the bias toward considering each suspicious political event as a separate case prevails even when those events are closely connected. For example, he suggests, despite obvious circumstantial evidence that John and Robert Kennedy were killed by the same people (right-wing US military and intelligence personnel backed by conservative oligarchs) for the same reasons (to maintain the Cold War in general and the Vietnam war in particular) the two assassinations are generally "seen as entirely unrelated" even by those who recognize them as inside jobs.[94]

Another series of apparent State Crimes Against Democracy (SCADS) that should be viewed as a coherent group, but often is not, is the subject of this chapter: The continuing progression of suspected false flag events serving as a public relations campaign for the so-called Global War on Terror (GWOT). From the questionable World Trade Center bombing of 1993, the "al-Qaeda" attacks on the US embassies in Dar es Salaam and Nairobi in 1998, the attack on the USS Cole in October 2000, to the subsequent false flag atrocities of 9/11-anthrax, Bali, Madrid, London, and Mumbai, to the Fort Hood shooter, the underwear bomber, the Boston Marathon bombing, the Times Square bomb attempt, the chemical weapons attack at al-Ghouta, Syria, and Islamic State atrocities and beheading videos, to the late 2014 through early 2015 attacks in Canada, Australia, France, and Denmark, the ongoing phenomenon of extremist, apparently strategically counterproductive terror attributed to radical Islam but sometimes performed or enabled by Western intelligence agencies and their privatized spin-offs, demands to be considered as a unified phenomenon, not a series of isolated events. Those who question any one of these alleged Islamic terror incidents in isolation are at a disadvantage in relation to the purveyors of the official story, who can draw on a larger narrative that synthesizes the whole series of events as examples of an alleged Islamist threat. For example, 9/11 truth-seekers are routinely challenged about other alleged Islamic extremist attacks, especially those that preceded 9/11, by defenders of the received notion of equating terrorism with radical Islam. The larger notion of a radical Islamist terror threat, for mainstream thinkers, has become a myth that conditions the interpretation of any specific event purporting to involve Islam and terrorism.

Because they have accepted the Islamic terror myth as a mode of interpreting reality that is ontologically superior to mere facts, defenders of the status quo are impervious to challenges questioning the empirical evidence supporting a conventional interpretation of any specific terror incident.

9/11- Anthrax: Lynchpin of a Terror Myth

The mythic interpretive template directing Americans to blame Muslims for terrorist incidents was hammered deep into public consciousness on September 11th, 2001.

Almost from the moment the Twin Towers were struck, TV news anchors, expert guests and political leaders began chanting the magic words "al-Qaeda" and "Bin Laden" despite the lack of evidence supporting such an interpretation.

The very next day, as if by magic, a list with 19 names of alleged radical Muslim hijackers materialized, supposedly discovered in Mohamed Atta's suitcase, which (we were told) had somehow failed to make the transfer between the commuter plane Atta took from Portland, Maine to Boston and the doomed Flight 11.[103]

Though the list of 19 names included two who died before 9/11 and ten who were alive after 9/11[95], and though Atta's suitcase included incompetently forged documents such as his supposed will beginning with a botched bismillah reading "In the name of God, myself and my family"[96] – and though the notion of Atta putting his will and a list of hijackers in a suitcase headed for oblivion makes even less sense than the story of his driving from Boston to Portland on September 10th so he would have to catch a commuter flight with a tight connection to Flight 11 – the absurdly improbable account was uncritically accepted by mainstream institutions including the media, the courts, Congress, and most of the academy.

Even when a former high-level intelligence official admitted to the *New Yorker* that the so-called evidence implicating the alleged hijackers was obviously planted, saying "Whatever trail was left was left deliberately—for the FBI to chase," mainstream investigative journalists were unwilling to dig deeper to discover who had planted the evidence and left the false trail.[97]

9/11-anthrax appears to have been designed to etch in stone the mythic template equating Islam and terrorism.[98] One year earlier, in September 2000, the neoconservative Zionists at Project for a New American Century had called for a "catastrophic and catalyzing event – like a New Pearl Harbor."[99]

As 9/11 Commission scriptwriter Philip Zelikow had written in a 1998 *Foreign Affairs* article envisioning a terrorist attack destroying the World Trade Center: "Like Pearl Harbor, this event would divide our past and future into a before and after."[100]
Zelikow, that self-described expert in the "creation and maintenance of public myths,"[101] knew that 9/11 or its equivalent would be remembered in the collective imagination as the kind of primordial event similar to the creation of the world in creation myths.

Such events are remembered as transformative catalysts that divide time into a nebulous long-ago-and-far-away "before" and an "after" that is the world as we know it. Zelikow and his fellow Zionist neocons also knew that the new world "after" 9/11 would be dominated by a mythic interpretive framework demonizing Muslims as terrorist enemies. After the creation of the public myth of Islamic terror via the "catastrophic and catalyzing event" of 9/11-anthrax, maintenance of that public myth could be performed by intermittently creating or publicizing smaller terror events.

Thus 9/11-anthrax played a central role in the creation of the Islamic terror myth. Prior to the autumn of 2001, such high profile but far-from-catalyzing events as the 1993 World Trade Center bombing, the African embassy bombings, and the USS Cole attack paved the road to 9/11-anthrax by creating a plausible enemy image on whom the coming "New Pearl Harbor" could be blamed. While space does not permit a detailed analysis of these three events, I will briefly summarize key points cited by those who argue for the false flag interpretation of the three major pre-9/11 alleged Islamic extremist attacks.

Pre-9/11 False Flags: Creating a Plausible Enemy

Compelling evidence indicates that the 1993 World Trade Center bombing, like 9/11, was an inside job. Such evidence includes testimony by an outraged Emad Salem, the FBI informant and agent provocateur who hatched the plot and directed its logistics, that the FBI had promised him that it would build a phony non-explosive bomb but "we didn't do that."[102]

As the *New York Times* reported: "'Do you deny,' Mr. Salem says he told the other agent, 'Your supervisor is the main reason for bombing the World Trade Center?' Mr. Salem said Mr. Anticev did not deny it."[103] Additionally, the official story that the FBI cracked the case when Mohammed A. Salameh, who had rented the truck used in the bombing, was arrested when he returned to the rental company to ask for his deposit back makes no sense.[104]

Like the 1993 World Trade Center bombing, the bombings of two US embassies in Tanzania and Kenya in 1998 appear to have been inside jobs facilitated by an American agent provocateur. The undercover American agent who arranged the African embassy bombings was US Army Sgt. Ali Mohamed.

Though the official cover story holds that Sgt. Mohamed infiltrated the US military on behalf of al-Qaeda rather than the other way around, the preponderance of evidence suggests the contrary. Mainstream investigative journalist Peter Lance, pretending to support the cover story while publishing evidence against it, reports:

> Ali Mohamed ... was something of an al Qaeda super-spy who managed to work with terrorists, the Green Berets, the CIA and become an FBI informant, even while ensuring Osama bin Laden's safe passage around the middle east. For years, Triple Cross alleges, the FBI and specifically [prosecutor Patrick] Fitzgerald, knew about him but allowed Mohamed's activities to continue unchecked.[105]

University of California professor Peter Dale Scott confirms that Sgt. Mohamed "worked for the FBI, the CIA, and U.S. Special Forces."[106] Scott reports that Sgt. Mohamed's FBI handler John Zent facilitated the African embassy bombings by telling the Royal Canadian Mounted Police to release Mohamed, who had been held as a terrorist suspect.[107] Scott cites numerous similar examples showing that Mohamed enjoyed official US government protection while carrying out his terrorist activities.

Like the 1993 and 1998 bombings, the October 2000 attack on the USS Cole in Yemen, which killed 17 sailors and wounded 49, appears to have been facilitated or orchestrated by corrupt US government officials. Handicapped teenager Tawfiq Bin Attash, publicly billed as a mastermind of the attack was in no position to succeed with his harebrained scheme of filling a dinghy with explosives and attacking the next American ship that passed by. Attash and his friends must have had professional inside help finding out when the USS Cole would be passing within range; their booby-trapped dinghy provided cover for a pre-planted explosion from within the ship that did most of the damage.

(The modus operandi echoed the false flag sinking of the USS Maine by a bomb planted inside the ship, blamed on a nonexistent Spanish attack from without.[108] In July 2001, the Yemeni government's investigation concluded that the American government had bombed its own ship as a pretext for military action of some kind, possibly including a planned invasion and occupation of the port of Aden.[109] But in retrospect, it seems that the overriding strategic purpose of the USS Cole bombing was to pave the road to 9/11-anthrax by hoisting the false flag of al-Qaeda to the level of plausible patsy.

Post-9/11 False Flags: Maintaining the Public Myth

Just as an intermittent series of relatively small false-flag attacks set the stage for 9/11-anthrax and its enshrinement of the Islamic terror myth, another series of relatively minor attacks since 2001 has kept the terror pot boiling. The first major 9/11-anthrax follow-up was the Bali bombing, which Australian journalist Joe Vialls argued was accomplished by an Israeli miniature nuclear weapon.[110] While this may come as news to consumers of the Western mainstream media, most Indonesians recognized the false flag from day one. As Sidney Jones reported in *The Observer* two weeks after the crime: "Absurd, as it may seem, if talk shows and media commentaries are any indications, the most likely candidates in most Indonesians' minds are the U.S. government and the Indonesian army."[111] The Indonesians were likely right. Eyewitness Dmitri Khalezov has testified that former Israeli Mossad chief Mike Harari was arrested in Thailand for orchestrating the Bali bombing, then released under pressure from foreign governments. Khalezov has provided documents supporting his assertion.[112] An American-supported Israeli mini-nuke attack has emerged as the most plausible scenario for the Bali attack.

The next spectacular international attack attributed to al-Qaeda was the Madrid train bombing of March 11th, 2004 – which, coincidentally or not, occurred exactly 911 days after 9/11. French journalist Mathieu Miquel, relying exclusively on official court documents and from Spanish mainstream media sources, reports: "As incredible as it may seem, the evidence that supposedly confirms the theory (that Islamists carried out the attacks) cannot stand up to rigorous analysis. And the suspicious behavior of certain elements of the police forces clearly indicates the existence of an intent to sabotage the investigation."[113] If the police framed innocent Muslims and sabotaged the investigation, the attack must have been yet another false flag designed to maintain the Islamic terror myth.

Then came the London mass transit bombings of July 7th, 2005. Once again, the official attempt to convict Islamist terrorists falls apart upon close inspection. Scholar and author Nafeez Ahmed has written a book raising questions about the official story,[114] while another British academician, Nick Kollerstrom, has written an even longer book demonstrating at length and in detail that the event was clearly a government-sponsored false flag attack and that the Muslim patsies were innocent.[115]

In November 2008 another spectacular, supposedly Muslim extremist attack occurred in Mumbai, India. Pakistani TV host and defense analyst Zaid Hamid has cited evidence that this attack, known in India as 26/11, was the product of Hindu extremists in Indian intelligence in collaboration with the Israeli Mossad.[116] It later emerged that a CIA agent named David Headley had orchestrated the attack.[117]

Headley apparently masterminded the attack on behalf of Zionist elements in US and Indian intelligence, with Mossad behind them, in order to falsely blame the attack on Pakistan: "Although American and Indian investigators have used David Headley in order to link him with Pakistan, yet his real connections are concerned with Indian secret agency RAW [India's most powerful intelligence agency] and American CIA."[118]

For simplicity's sake, I will focus for the remainder of this overview of post-9/11 synthetic terror on the USA, the would-be unipolar world hegemon whose acceptance of the Islamic terror myth is most crucial to the neoconservative-Zionist program.

After a hiatus lasting most of the decade, the false flag of Islamic terror was re-hoisted in the USA following the Fort Hood shootings of November 2009. (Technically this event cannot be classified under the terrorism rubric since the victims were soldiers, not civilians.) American historian and terror analyst Webster Tarpley writes that the Fort Hood massacre attributed to Major Nidal Hasan unleashed "an articulated campaign of media hysteria and mass manipulation."[119]

Tarpley went on to question the official story of the shootings by citing reports of multiple shooters, adding: "There remains the question of whether Major Hasan's psychosis has been artificially produced through a program of brainwashing and heavy-duty 'Clockwork Orange' psychological manipulation." That question would re-emerge in 2014 in connection to another likely Manchurian Candidate terrorist, the leader of Islamic State and self-proclaimed Caliph Abu Bakr al-Baghdadi.

If the Fort Hood shooting was tragic, the follow-up incident involving a so-called underwear bomber was pure farce. While the American people were told that a terrorist named Umar Farouk Abdulmutallab had packed his underwear full of plastic explosives in hope of blowing up a jetliner, they were not told that Abdulmutallab did not have a detonator—and that plastic explosives cannot explode without a detonator.

Worse, eyewitnesses saw Abdulmutallab boarding the Detroit-bound plane in Amsterdam without a passport, escorted by a "sharply-dressed man" who appeared to be some sort of security agent. A cameraman on board the plane was clearly complicit in the attack, beginning to film shortly before the attack began, and panning seamlessly to capture the entire episode as if on cue.

Passenger and eyewitness Kurt Haskell, a Detroit attorney, has published convincing evidence that the whole affair was a poorly disguised false flag operation.[120]

ABC News reported Haskell's courtroom testimony: "I am convinced that Umar was given an intentionally defective bomb by a U.S. agent to stage a false terrorist attack."[126]

A subsequent headline-garnering reminder of the alleged Islamic terror threat was the Times Square bombing attempt of May 1st, 2010. Like the underwear bombing incident, the Times Square scare involved an utterly incompetent terrorist patsy and a so-called bomb that was highly unlikely to explode. According to former US intelligence insider Gordon Duff, editor of Veterans Today, the fake attack was "part of a CIA false flag against Pakistan."[121]

The next major American myth-maintenance operation was the Boston Marathon bombing of April 2013. If anything, this alleged Islamic terror incident was an even more crushingly obvious false flag than its predecessors. Photographs taken at the scene show that the exploded backpack the FBI claims held a bomb was not worn by either Tsarnaev brother, but instead by an unknown man wearing a cap with insignia of Craft International, a Blackwater-style outfit owned by "American Sniper" Chris Kyle specializing in mercenary mayhem whose motto is "Sometimes violence *does* solve problems."

Craft and the officials who hired them hid from the media and refused to either deny or explain the mercenaries' presence at the Marathon.[122] Video taken at the scene reveals apparently staged carnage complete with theatrical pseudo-amputations of artificial limbs and poorly distributed amounts of cinematic fake blood.[123]

The FBI murdered a key witness, Ibrahim Todashev, execution style while he was in custody.[124] The Tsarnaevs' uncle Ruslan Tsarnaev was married to Samantha Fuller, daughter of notorious CIA agent Graham Fuller, until 2004.[125]
Graham Fuller has allegedly been implicated in a number of scandals including the Iran-Contra affair and the creation of al-Qaeda.[126] He provided support to Chechens fighting against Russia.[132]

Fuller has advocated "guiding the evolution of Islam" and has been called the CIA controller for the ethnic Turkish USA-based Fethullah Gulen organization which controls over $20 billion in assets and has been accused of trying to overthrow the government of Turkey.[127] While in Turkey in May 2011 I met with leading Turkish journalists who said Fuller, who headed the CIA station in that country in September 2001, threatened them and told them not to question the official story of 9/11 in print.

In a February 20th, 2015, email to this author, Fuller derided the allegations, saying "My voluminous writings over the years make abundantly clear what my position is on a wealth of issues and my consistent criticisms of US policies; these ridiculous allegations are simply utterly inconsistent with what I say, do or write."
Given his opposition to neoconservative-driven Islamophobia, it is conceivable that Fuller has been slandered by neocon operatives, and that the accusations against him are baseless or exaggerated.

With or without Graham Fuller, think tanks and covert operations professionals have certainly "guided the evolution of Islam" not only by propping up such "moderate Muslim" Zionist apologists as Fethullah Gulen, but also by promoting the appalling and repulsive sectarian cruelty of so-called Islamic State, formerly known as ISIS or ISIL. This extremist group, which primarily attacks Muslims and to a lesser extent Christians as it destabilizes Israel's potential enemies, was armed and trained at CIA bases in Jordan and unleashed against the Syrian government of President Bashar al-Assad and later Iraq.[128]

According to an American mainstream media report that has been scrubbed from the internet, as well as numerous Iraqi reports, pretender to the caliphate Abu Bakr al-Baghdadi was held by US forces at Camp Bucca at least four years despite official denials.[129]

The official attempt to cover up al-Baghdadi's four-year stay at Camp Bucca suggests that the self-styled caliph may have been enlisted or even mind-controlled while in US custody.[130] The preponderance of evidence suggests that Zionist elements of US-NATO manufactured ISIS not only to destabilize Israel's potential enemies but also to maintain the public myth of Islamic terror and the clash of civilizations it spawned.

The Emerging Counter-Narrative

By considering the above series of high-profile false flag attacks attributed to Muslims as a coherent phenomenon, rather than a series of isolated events, we are preparing the ground for an emerging counter-narrative challenging the myth of Islamic terror. This counter-narrative begins with the observation that no rational American should fear terrorism of any kind since it poses a threat to human life and limb far below the level of lightning strikes and bathtub drownings.[131]

It continues with the observation that according to the American FBI, only 6% of terrorist attacks on American soil are even attributed (whether correctly or incorrectly) to radical Muslims, who statistically pose less of a terror threat than radical Jews, leftists, or Hispanics – despite imbalanced media coverage suggesting the contrary.[132] Finally, it asks who created and promoted the false notion of an Islamic terrorist threat, and for what ends...and answers the question by pointing to neoconservative Zionists, whose political philosophy is based on the need for an enemy, whether actual or mythical.[144]

In the absence of a coherent counter-narrative, those questioning the official story of any alleged terror attack are at a serious disadvantage. A high-level aide to George W. Bush, reputed to be Karl Rove, famously suggested to journalist Ron Suskind that artificially created public myths have superseded empirical reality:

The aide said that guys like me were "in what we call the reality-based community," which he defined as people who "believe that solutions emerge from your judicious study of discernible reality." I nodded and murmured something about enlightenment principles and empiricism. He cut me off. "That's not the way the world really works anymore." He continued "We're an empire now, and when we act, we create our own reality. And while you're studying that reality—judiciously, as you will—we'll act again, creating other new realities, which you can study too, and that's how things will sort out. We're history's actors ... and you, all of you, will be left to just study what we do."[145]

While narratives can certainly take leave from reality, especially when fabricated by liars, they can also serve as honest efforts to communicate reality. The reality-based community should recognize the power of narrative and fight back against the empire of lies by telling truthful stories that outstrip the false ones promulgated by political hacks.

And perhaps the most important truthful counter-narrative available today is the above-sketched revisionist account of the so-called War on Terror.

NO PLANES ON 911 – THE TWO-MINUTE VIDEO

By Ronald Bleier

May 2015

Editor's Notes

By 2015, I had long since given up hoping for the miracle that would expose the illusion of planes and hijackers on 9/11 in a manner that would be politically significant. I was reconciled to the reality that Oliver Stone's breakthrough movie *JFK* (1991) would not be repeated and that there would be no independent investigation revisiting the events of 9/11. Nevertheless, in the years after my 2006 "No Planes" article, I learned more about cell phone calls and the difficulties (or impossibilities) of inexperienced Arab pilots flying airliners into NYC skyscrapers. And so, when I saw the CNN two-minute video, I decided to revisit the NPT.

By then I also wanted to record my bitter disillusionment with President Obama. Even before the end of his first year in office, I had been shocked and dismayed that he had entered office intending to continue and expand the ruthless permanent war agenda made possible by the 9/11 hoax. Even worse was that he didn't have Bush and Cheney's ideological excuse. For them, war and destruction were their means of ordering the world to their satisfaction. But Obama knew better. He knew that permanent war would not be in the short or long-term interest of the U.S. and the world. I had to conclude that for Obama, the point was devastation, suffering and chaos.

To successfully implement his agenda of ruin, President Obama intended to rid himself of the constraints of his party's control of Congress. By insisting, for example, on bailing out Wall Street, and doing nothing for Main Street, he energized Republican opposition and sidelined his base, ensuring the loss of the House in 2010. He was doubtless unhappy that it took him longer, until November 2014, to switch control of the Senate to the Republicans.

In line with his permanent war agenda, President Obama slow-walked the release of the Guantanamo prisoners, ensuring that the prison in Cuba would remain open indefinitely. He refused due process for 40 – 50 of the so-called "worst of the worst" prisoners, despite his evident knowledge that they were not guilty of anything connected to 9/11. His administration had unrestricted access to their personnel files and so could see, if they wished, that the only evidence against these prisoners were their confessions under torture.

Another sign of the continuation of the Global War on Terror on Obama's watch was the "assassination" in May 2011 of al-Qaeda mastermind, Osama bin Laden. The previous administration had left President-elect Barack Obama with a public relations conundrum since Bin Laden had been reliably reported dead seven years earlier. On December 26, 2001, Fox News picked up notice of Bin Laden's demise from the Egyptian newspaper *Al Wafd* with no contradiction from his inner circle. Nevertheless the Bush administration, in due course, "resurrected" him for political reasons.

It was no secret that by the end of 2001, although only 44, Bin Laden was deathly ill. In his last authenticated video, the so-called post-November 16 [2001] video, he appeared gaunt and frail, his beard whiter than ever.

Consistent with having suffered a stroke, he was unable to move his left arm. In connection with Bin Laden's December 2001 death, public statements from any number of public figures like Defense Secretary Donald Rumsfeld, Oliver North, and Pakistani President Pervez Musharraf suggested the probability or certainty that he had died. (According to reports, President Bush also privately wondered the same thing.) Rumsfeld also acknowledged that after December 2001, U.S. surveillance, which had been monitoring Bin Laden's substantial cell phone traffic, picked up no further communications from him.[133]

In order to "kill" an already dead man, the Obama administration concocted a high-profile Navy Seal raid in May 2011 at his alleged compound in Abbottabad, northeastern Pakistan. Unsurprisingly the U.S. offered no proof they had killed anyone. No DNA or post-mortem photographs were produced. Making verification impossible, they claimed to have dropped his "body" into the North Arabian Sea.

***

Part 1 - The Two-Minute Video

--Do you have two minutes to look at a video?
CNN Flight 175 Slow Motion
https://www.youtube.com/watch?v=B7UtX_QoSdY

A

s soon I saw "Flight 175 – Slow Motion Video," a two-minute video on YouTube (h/t JG) regarding the strike on the South World Trade Center Tower on 9/11, I realized that I had finally found a vehicle -- and the magic words -- that would get the attention of friends and family.

Since the video was only two minutes long I was able to approach people whom I suspected would otherwise balk at entertaining conspiracy theories, especially on this topic.

The video supplied me with the magic words: "Do you have two minutes to look at a video?"

It worked beautifully. Reactions more than fulfilled even my optimistic hopes. Virtually everyone in the handful of people to whom I showed it was profoundly affected. Viewers were thrown into confusion if not outright disbelief about the government's version of what happened that day. After watching the video, as often as not, a conversation ensued about the implications of what was seen.

The First Anomaly Summarized

As the video title — "Flight 175 – Slow Motion Video" — indicates, we see, in "super slow motion" –the purported United Airlines flight 175 passenger jet crashing into the South Tower on 9/11. The narrator/producer, Kevin Walsh, an independent researcher, announces that by slowing down the video he's going to point to two "impossibilities."

The first impossibility is that when the "plane" strikes the building, we see that it doesn't break up into pieces as might be expected but disappears and is swallowed up into the building. But this is a physical impossibility. As Walsh puts it: "a real airplane couldn't have sliced through a building with a steel façade with reinforced concrete flooring, with 47 steel support beams. A jet's wing can't slice through a steel building like a hot knife through butter."

9/11 activist, Morgan Reynolds, author and chief economist in the Bush administration (2001-2002), helps explain why a jet plane could not be swallowed up by a steel tower. The key is that the fuselage of an airplane is relatively fragile.

"With only minor hyperbole," he writes, a plane's fuselage is essentially "a hollow aluminum tube." Compared to the weight of the building -- half a million tons — vs. the weight of the plane – 140 tons – "the plane, of course, would be crushed."

> Among large jetliner components, only engines and landing gear would retain serious structural integrity in a collision although small parts like actuators would remain intact too. ...[P]lanes running into *mountains*,..., concrete barriers, and steel buildings *fare* very poorly, just as speeding *automobiles* hitting a ... telephone *pole* or *tree* do. A plane flying into a WTC tower should break up, shatter and scatter pieces everywhere.[134]

The Second Impossibility

Walsh explains that the second impossibility is in plain sight – pun apparently intended – though he says with chagrin that the anomaly is sufficiently subtle that it took him almost twelve years to spot it. He begins with a still picture and points to a building that's clearly behind the South Tower. Walsh explains that if the video was what it was purported to be, a real amateur video credited to Michael Hezarkhani, a diamond merchant from Los Angeles, the wing of the plane, as it moves toward the Tower, would appear **in front of** the background building. As the video proceeds, we see that the plane's wing appears **behind the building,** not in front of it. Something is wrong.

Walsh calls this a "glitch," a layering CGI (Computer Generated Image) "glitch." Once it's pointed out, it's so obviously a glaring mistake that it seems immediately evident that the video is fake. My brief experience showing Walsh's video to a few family members and friends indicated that it is this second anomaly of the wing appearing in the wrong place is the one that most persuasively exposes the scam.

Complacency and Fear

As it happens, I'm an atheist so I don't believe in God, nor do I believe in alien abductions, or shape-shifting Illuminati. However, if someone presented me with the opportunity to spend two minutes looking at what they claimed was evidence for the existence of any of these phenomena, I suspect I wouldn't mind taking that much time out of my busy schedule to satisfy myself or to please my informant.

Yet I suspect my willingness to look at such evidence arises from my confidence that nothing I could be shown in two minutes – or two hours – could rock my world or my worldview. But what if someone were to offer me the opportunity to look at evidence that I actually feared might overturn my belief system, the means by which I manage to control and navigate in my own little world? Would I have the courage to spend two minutes looking at such evidence?

Question:

Can you spare two minutes to look at a video?
"CNN Flight 175 Slow Motion"

Part 2 - My Journey to No planes on 9/11

F

or about three years I believed the official story of 9/11 – I believed that fanatical, enraged Muslims used planes as weapons to bring down the Twin Towers – and all the rest of the 9/11 fable. What I lacked that day was someone who might have explained that steel-framed buildings do not, cannot and never have been brought down by fires, no matter how large or intense.

It wasn't until 2004 that my belief in the official story was overturned by watching a one-hour presentation on controlled demolition by 9/11 researcher Jim Hoffman.[135]

From Hoffman's talk and from other videos on 9/11 research, I learned that for a tall building to collapse at the speed of gravity – less than 10 seconds in the case of the Twin Towers – the intervening resistance must be removed. For example, the resistance provided by floor 89 must be removed before floor 90 can fall freely, and so on. The only way this can be accomplished is by controlled demolition, where software can coordinate the removal of resistance by means of explosives. I agreed with Hoffman's conclusion that 9/11 must have been an inside job since Osama Bin Laden could not have arranged for controlled demolition.

 A prominent real-world example of even massive fire unable to cause the collapse of tall buildings was the One Meridian Plaza fire in Philadelphia in 1991 which burned for 18 hours and was described by local officials as "the most significant fire in this century." Other such examples include the First Interstate Fire (1988), the One New York Plaza Fire (1970), the Caracas Tower Fire (2004) and the even more severe Windsor Building Fire (2005). Sufficiently hot fire above 2500 F – not the relatively small fires which were quickly going out on 9/11 -- will cause steel to melt and bend but will not remove the intervening resistance from floor to floor leading to collapse.[136]

Hoffman's convincing presentation stimulated me to seek additional information about what really happened on 9/11. I found an authoritative voice regarding anomalies in the official story of 9/11 in books by Professor David Ray Griffin. Known by his fans as the Guru of 9/11, he has written at least eleven books on the subject. After reading his first two books, *The New Pearl Harbor* (2004) and *The 9/11 Commission Report: Omissions and Distortions* (2005), I was convinced that 9/11 was an inside job.

Griffin's clear and eloquent prose offered persuasive evidence that reinforced my understanding that since OBL and fanatical Muslims could not have arranged for controlled demolition, the only logical deduction must be that the 9/11 terror attacks must have been planned and executed by the U.S. government, masterminded, I concluded, by Dick Cheney, George W. Bush, Donald Rumsfeld, et al.

Their motive: they intended to jump-start their permanent war agenda via the "war on terror," beginning with the invasions of Afghanistan and Iraq.

I learned that the term "a new Pearl Harbor" – which Griffin used as the title of his first book on 9/11 -- was coined in the 1997 founding document of the neoconservative Project for a New American Century (PNAC). The phrase symbolized and encapsulated their stated objective to and to maintain a high level of military spending despite the end of the Cold War. They hoped to affect a "revolutionary" program of unprecedented U.S. global dominance through unbounded militarism and aggression. They had the chutzpah to write that an extraordinary terror event would be necessary to "catalyze" the drastic change in the political culture — to move America off its complacent course as they saw it, into a new world of endless aggression.

As they put it: "the process of transformation, even if it brings revolutionary change, is likely to be a long one, absent some catastrophic and catalyzing event—like a new Pearl Harbor."

No Planes on 9/11?! Some of the Evidence

About a year after I was convinced that 9/11 was an inside job, an email from a colleague pointed me to "the best single article on 9/11." My friend's praise turned out not to be hyperbole.

I was soon convinced by Gerard Holmgren's ten-page article "Manufactured Terrorism – The Truth About Sept 11," (2004,) — that no planes were involved in the 9/11 attacks. Holmgren's article was also the stimulus for a follow-up article by Morgan Reynolds, author and chief economist in the Bush administration (2001-2002),

"We Have Some Holes in the Plane Stories," (March 2006). Reynolds's article added gravitas and more detail to the theory and the two articles made a powerful, credible case.

Among their strongest points is one similar to the first of the anomalies pointed out by Kevin Walsh's video: if a plane with a mostly aluminum body was to strike a tall building it wouldn't be swallowed up by the building: it would break up and parts of the planes would fall to the ground. The steel jet engines would survive in recognizable form and wreckage of all types would be available for independent verification. A real plane crash would leave behind body parts, seat cushions, luggage, and similar evidence, but none has ever been produced for any of the 9/11 alleged passenger plane crashes. A terrible recent real-world example of evident post-crash debris is the wreckage visible in media photos of the remains of the Germanair crash in the French Alps in March 2015.)

John Lear, a celebrated professional pilot, who retired after 40 years of flying including experience with flying jets of all types, the grandson of William Lear, the inventor of, the Learjet, has lambasted the official account of 9/11. In a 2011 affidavit, he flatly asserts that no Boeing 787 struck the Twin Towers because such a thing would have been "physically impossible. Lear cited the crucial absence of verifiable plane wreckage. With regard to Flight 175 – the same flight as in the Walsh video – he argues that "a real Boeing 767 would have begun 'telescoping' "when it struck the steel framed building. "The vertical and horizontal tail would have instantaneously separated from the aircraft, hit the steel box columns and fallen to the ground."

Lear agrees also with Reynolds that the 9,000-pound engines would have survived such a crash and "either fallen to the ground or been recovered in the debris of the collapsed building. ... Normal operating temperatures for these engines are 650°C so they could not possibly have burned up."

Lear contends that if the nose of an airplane crashed into such a building, "the momentum of the wings would have slowed drastically depriving them of the energy to penetrate the exterior steel box columns." Furthermore, the "spars of the wing, which extend outward, could not possibly have penetrated the 14-inch by 14-inch steel box columns placed 39 inches on center and would have crashed to the ground."

In another article, Reynolds argues that the 'unprecedented collapses in steel framed skyscrapers, bear all the hallmarks of demolition – virtual free fall speed of collapse, pulverization of concrete … film and photographic evidence of explosions." Reynolds dismisses theories that anything other than explosives caused the WTC collapse. "In sporting parlance, the contest between two rival scientific theories produced a rout: demolition 100, impact-fire-pancake-collapse theory 0. The official 'pancake' story cannot account for the wide range of incontestable facts involved in the collapses while demolition can." [137]

Holmgren directs attention to the contradiction between the almost instant claim that Osama bin Laden was responsible, and the surprise of the Bush administration at the attacks and the apparent inaction and disinterest of President Bush and Acting Chairman of the Joint Chiefs of Staff, General Richard Myers, during the attacks. Holmgren points to the immediate threat to invade Afghanistan when it turned out the decision to do so had already been made by July 2001 and the plans were on Bush's desk by Sept 9; and the urban myth that Bin Laden claimed responsibility for the attacks.

It's also an urban myth that Osama bin Laden (OBL) took responsibility for the 9/11 terror. There is plenty of evidence that he immediately denied such smears. High on Google's first page of their list of more than 280,000 hits for a search for "Osama bin Laden denies his involvement in 9/11" is the CNN story six days after 9/11 where OBL is quoted as saying: "I would like to assure the world that I did not plan the recent attacks, which seems to have been planned by people for personal reasons." CNN is careful to get President Bush's response. "No question he [OBL] is the prime suspect. No question about that."

Where Are the Arabs?

Holmgren wonders how credible it was that the FBI was able to so quickly identify 19 Arab hijackers within a few days.

Similarly, he is skeptical about the allegation that passports of some of the hijackers as well as suicide notes were found at the crash sites. He also found it "miraculous" that the luggage of the purported ringleader, Mohammed Atta just happened to be left for the FBI to find at Logan airport. Luckily, he writes, the FBI also found Atta's written instructions to his fellow hijackers.

More reason for skepticism appeared when some of the alleged hijackers began turning up alive after 9/11 and denying any part in terror activity. Nor were there any Arabic names on the passenger lists provided by the airlines. Circumstantial evidence that no hijackings occurred, was that "not in not one of the four alleged hijackings did any of the crew punch in the four-digit hijacking code to alert Air Traffic Control." Holmgren also wonders why there was no distress call from Flight AA 11 (which allegedly struck the North Tower) when there was a purported 25-minute standoff, including the shooting and stabbing of passengers.[138]

More important work researching the lack of evidence for hijackers has been done by Elias Davidsson, author of *Hijacking America's Mind on 9/11: Counterfeiting Evidence* (2013). At some length, he pulls together evidence gathered over the years that there is no authenticated CCTV video of the hijackers at the departure gates; there are no authenticated passenger lists or boarding passes; there has been no positive identification of the hijacker's bodily remains; nor are there any witnesses who have seen the hijackers at the security and boarding pass checkpoints.

Impugning Muslims

In the case of 9/11, the "key to acquiescence in the government's war on terror and global domination project is public belief in Arab hijacked airliners and crashes," writes Morgan Reynolds.

The pivotal place for Muslim responsibility for 9/11 explains some of the "intense resistance" to the theory of No Planes. Arab/Muslim culpability for this extraordinary terror event fortuitously supports the Israeli-Zionist agenda of viewing the Islamic world as an existential threat and helps to ensure pro-Zionist support for the official story. It's difficult to imagine the planners of 9/11 going forward had it been the other way around: had the official story challenged the Zionist, anti-Muslim agenda.

Practical Difficulties with Planes

Holmgren takes up some of the practical difficulties of actually pulling off the 9/11 attacks by means of passenger jets. For example, the planners would have to choose between using suicide pilots or piloting the jets by remote control. He writes that the difficulties of using real pilots are not difficult to imagine.

> What if, for example, the Arab pilots haven't been trained to fly jets? Or if they haven't been trained to fly jets without responding to ground control? What if they don't wake up in time to make their flights? Eric Hufschmid, an advocate of the theory that the passenger jets were piloted by remote control asks similar questions: "What if the hijackers decide to switch from hitting the World

What about the option of remotely controlling the planes -- which some researchers believe gets around the unlikelihood of U.S. officials coordinating with Muslim terrorists to drive planes into tall buildings? Holmgren writes that the option of using remotely controlled planes either with or without passengers runs into

"potentially insurmountable problems with the cover-up."

A remotely controlled plane might "hit some other building, just clip its wing on the tower and crash into the streets or cause a cascade of damage on other non-targeted buildings, miss altogether and finish up in the Hudson ..."

To the planners of 9/11, even the smallest risk of missing the target exactly would be unacceptable, writes Holmgren, since difficulties with the alternative scenario – perhaps employing cruise missiles, for example – would be "easily manageable."

Holmgren suggests some of the problems that the planners might envision. "For example, an unacceptable outcome would be if the plane missed or slightly missed its target, and it was found that there were no passengers. Similarly, if there were passengers and one or more survived to tell their story. Even if no passengers survived, innocent rescue workers might arrive before the cover-up crew and discover and release forensic evidence inimical to the cover story."[139] Holmgren argues that any of these outcomes would be "far worse" than the relatively negligible risk involved with potentially contradictory witness testimony in the "18 minutes between the two tower strikes."

Media: The Key to the Official Story Fortress

If the circumstantial evidence against the official 9/11 theory is so strong, how does one explain its popularity and its durability? Although none of those responsible for 9/11 has come forward and no smoking gun documentation has as yet come to light, circumstantial evidence is routinely accepted as the basis for prosecution and for guilty verdicts.

The reason the official story continues to be so durable, it seems, is that most people will tend, as I did, to accept the government's version when it is backed up by the media. Since we rely so strongly on the government for our security and the stability of our system, we tend not to seek out or take seriously contradictory scenarios.

Especially in such dramatic, high profile, high stakes cases, when there is a media consensus, a magic circle, a fortress of allowable discourse, is created so that skeptics tend to be marginalized or invisible.

When Lee Harvey Oswald, the alleged murderer of President John F. Kennedy was murdered two days later on live television while in police custody, many instantly suspected that he was shot in order to prevent the exposure of a conspiracy. Such a shocking and blatant silencing of an indispensable witness was so obviously scandalous that it seemed a certainty that it would be followed up vigorously by the media and other high-profile politicians and others. But in the succeeding days and weeks, there was no such follow-up and no outcry developed. As a result, in time the public was lulled into complacency and fell back on reliance upon the government's account. An impenetrable magic circle developed around the official story about the JFK assassination which has lasted – in a respectable discourse on both the left and right -- to this day.

Is the Slow-Motion Video a Fake?

Two of the dozen or so people to whom I showed the Walsh video wondered aloud if it were certain that he could be trusted 100%. Was it not fair to ask if a 9/11 activist like Walsh might be manipulating his audience by altering key images? The answer to such a question would seem straightforward and easily dealt with by viewing the original CNN video, available on YouTube -- Twin Towers Attack [CNN] - 911 Plane crash;

Comparing the Walsh video with the CNN video will convince many that the Walsh video is genuine, that Walsh has simply slowed down the CNN video just as he represents. Yet some might still complain that the real-time CNN video proceeds too quickly to observe Walsh's first impossibility -- that the building has swallowed the plane and closed up afterward without a trace of damage. The building's absorption of the plane simply can't be seen in real-time.

Is (the lack of) Plane Wreckage Decisive?!

By replaying the early part of the CNN video -- seconds 6-12 -- as the plane strikes the building, viewers can see that the crash yields no visible evidence of plane wreckage falling to the ground or stuck into the building. No independently verifiable evidence of plane wreckage has ever been produced. Morgan Reynolds believes the question of wreckage is pretty close to decisive.

> The most obvious defect of the official story is the **absence or near-absence of conventional airplane wreckage** at each crash site. The government could have ended the controversy over planes long ago by allowing independent investigators to examine part numbers and compare them to each plane's maintenance logbook. This did not happen following the 9/11 crashes. (My emphasis)

Reynolds adds that it is actually difficult to find proof that airplanes crashed on 9/11 since "no air accident investigations were conducted," The government's theory apparently, is that since there is no doubt that the events of 9/11 were caused by Muslim terrorists, there was no need to proceed with air accident investigations.

Rebutting Walsh?

It didn't take long to find an online rebuttal to the Walsh video entitled, "9/11 WTC Second Plane - Michael Hezarkhani Footage - NOT FAKED by one Thomas David Dilley (thomasdavidlilleytdl). Dilley speaks with a British accent and provides a photo of a goateed young man, perhaps in his late 20s. At first, I wondered if he was an independent activist or a government-sponsored disinformation agent.

He claims that Walsh's second impossibility, the apparent layering CGI mistake of a wing appearing behind a building that is itself behind the South Tower, is NOT actually a mistake. He claims that the wing is really in the right place because if you look from another angle, *the building supposedly behind* the South Tower is really in front of it. Therefore, he concludes that the (CNN) Hezarkani video is not faked because the wing is really in the right place.

I had little difficulty dismissing the Dilley video as witting or unwitting disinformation. His argument seemed, after I thought about it for a bit, deliberately confusing. It's hard to imagine a building behind another from one view, and in front of the same building from another view.

In the end, I wondered whether whoever might be behind it considered that they might unintentionally be lending Walsh support by tacitly granting that his was indeed a bona fide slow-motion copy of the CNN video.

I also noted that the Dilley video didn't address the way the "plane" was absorbed by the building and closed up afterward – which can only be seen when the video is slowed down; nor does Dilley address the question of the lack of evidence of plane wreckage.

Part 3 - Controlled Demolition Means No Planes

Critical to my understanding of 9/11 as an inside job has been, what I believe is incontrovertible evidence for controlled demolition – steel high-rise buildings cannot fall at the speed of gravity into their own footprints absent controlled demolition. They never have done so before or since.

While working on this paper, I was startled to belatedly realize that those like me who believe that the Twin Towers (as well as Building 7) were brought down by controlled demolition should ALSO by default understand that no planes were involved in the 9/11 events since both at the same time requires the unrealistic scenario of the White House and other U.S. intelligence and security agencies coordinating with Muslim hijackers. If it were the case that the U.S. had planned to bring down three tall buildings in NYC via controlled demolition it was hard to imagine agents of Vice President Dick Cheney on the phone to Mohammed Atta, warning him not to indulge in his usual routine of night clubs, alcohol and women the evening before his big day.[140]

It's not that U.S. government agents don't routinely traffic with "terrorists" – those willing for money or ideology to take up assignments involving civilian terror and other mayhem. Rather, in an operation like 9/11 where all the damage was clearly handled in-house via controlled demolition, it makes no sense to depend in any way on outside elements.

My view of the incompatibility of employing both planes and controlled demolition was corroborated by a high-profile critic of the official story who even while he embraced the controlled demolition theory, nevertheless insisted on planes crashing into the Twin Towers. He resolved the difficulty with the theory that the passenger planes were remotely controlled. I took what I found to be his lame and unsatisfactory solution as a tacit admission of his view that in the real world there would have been no coordination between U.S. officials and Muslim hijackers.

I later recalled that years earlier the late great left journalist, activist, and author, Alexander Cockburn pointed out that the planes were just a distraction. He reasoned that if the Towers were brought down by controlled demolition, planes were unnecessary.

To be sure, Cockburn was writing from the perspective of someone SUPPORTING the official government theory because he was opposed to conspiracy theory on principle. His point about the planes as a distraction was intended as a rebuttal to those – in the great majority of the 9/11 research movement -- who still strongly maintain controlled demolition AND hijacked passenger planes. I suppose they maintain this (illogical?) position because they fear they will be discredited even in the ranks of their own supporters, not to mention outsiders.

I had anecdotal evidence that it was for political rather than evidentiary reasons that many 9/11 truthers insisted on both controlled demolition and planes when one of my 9/11 activist colleagues admitted as much to me years ago. Far more optimistic than I was at the time that 9/11 activism would actually lead to a media and political breakthrough, he allowed how he feared that embracing no planes would damage the 9/11 truth movement. In a perhaps happy ending, it turned out that it was this same colleague who recently emailed me the link to the Walsh video along with his report that this video helped convert him to No Planes.

Cockburn's view is characteristic of the anarchists/Marxist systemic critique of capitalism and imperialism which holds that individuals are merely weeds tossed about on history's great tides. Such a position seems to be the basis for Chomsky's (in) famous statement that the assassination of JFK was relatively insignificant because he was "just a man" – meaning that the blame should rather fall on the entire corrupt system and not on conspiracy theories that require specific individuals as the forces that can change history.

As David Ray Griffin has written in *The New Pearl Harbor,* it's not clear why a systemic critique should not be compatible with an understanding that actors in positions of power also can change history.

But our post-9/11 history has taught us that there is also a price to pay for accepting uncritically self-serving stories by the government and the media. Too many millions have already paid their terrible price in death, destruction and suffering and the future only seems bleaker for many more millions. Even in relatively untouched countries, government encroachment on liberty and privacy are ominous signs of a loss of democratic protections and a drift toward totalitarian control.

Inexperienced Pilots

On the day of 9/11, I readily accepted the notion that fanatical Muslim pilots had the operational skills to steer a passenger jet plane into the Twin Towers. Years later, I was to learn that such a thing was impossible in practice. I learned that the technical impediments were such that even the most skilled jet pilots could not routinely manage.

John Lear, the grandson of Bill Lear, the founder of the Lear Jet, is an experienced pilot in all types of aircraft, with 40 years, and 19,000 hours of flying time -- the majority spent on 3 or 4 jet engines -- confirms that even he couldn't do it without practice. The lack of a realistic basis for the government theory that planes crashed into the Twin Towers was compounded when we learned that the alleged pilots of September 11th, were amateurs, trained only on small propeller planes whose proficiency on these planes was judged "average" or "poor."

Some of the Hurdles of Using a Plane as a Weapon

In 2008 John Lear filed an affidavit in support of a lawsuit brought by Dr. Morgan Reynolds challenging the government theory "as to how and why the World Trade Center buildings collapsed on 9/11." Although the lawsuit was dismissed "with prejudice,"[141]

Lear's affidavit provides striking practical and technical details explaining how difficult it is in practice to steer a passenger plane from a cruising altitude of 35,000 ft into a tall city building. Lear believes it "would have been impossible...for anyone with little or no time in a Boeing 767...to have taken over and then flown the aircraft at high speed, then descend to below a thousand feet above sea level and then flown a course to impact the twin towers."

Why is it so difficult? Lear begins with the government theory is that the hijacker(s) would have to murder the pilot with a box knife. In that case, he points out, "there would be blood all over the seat, the controls, the center pedestal, the instrument panel and floor of the cockpit." The dead pilot would have been removed, the seat would have to be adjusted, spreading more blood over the controls and throttle, making them stickier and more difficult to operate."

After disposing somehow of the pilot(s), the hijackers would have been confronted with an 'EFIS' (Electronic Flight Instrumentation System) display panel, with its several screens and clusters of hard instruments. Lear finds it hard to imagine how an amateur would be able to interpret the display panel if they had not had the requisite training. How would such a pilot use the controls, "including the ailerons, rudder, elevators, spoilers and throttles to effect, control and maintain a descent? The Boeing 767 does not fly itself nor does it automatically correct any misuse of the controls."

> Even on a clear day, a novice pilot would be wholly incapable of taking control and turning a Boeing 767 towards New York because of his total lack of experience and situational awareness under these conditions. The alleged hijackers were not 'instrument rated' and controlled high-altitude flight requires experience in constantly referring to and cross-checking attitude, altitude and speed instruments. Using the distant horizon to fly 'visually' ... is virtually impossible, particularly at the cruising speed of the Boeing 767.

The next difficulty Lear addresses is the irritating clacking sound that would have sounded in the cockpit as soon as the airspeed went above 360 knots (=414 mph) since such speeds exceeds FAA guidelines. This clacker could not be turned off on 9/11/2001 but has since been changed since it interferes with pilot decision-making. The clacker and speed of the airplane figures in the Lear affidavit because the government version explains the lack of wreckage due to the high speed of the Boeing jets of more than 500 mph crashing into a steel-framed building, thereby crushing all the wreckage into invisibility.

Last Moments of Flight

Another reason a hijacker would have difficulty finding a relatively straight course into New York City was "because of the difficulty of controlling heading, descent rate and descent speed ..." And what would happen, Lear wonders, after the pilot has managed to effectively use the 67 seconds it would have taken at 790 ft per second to navigate the last ten miles to NYC? At that point, he would have had "to line up perfectly with a 208 ft wide target ... and stay lined up with the clacker clacking plus the tremendous air noise against the windshield and the bucking bronco-like airplane."
The added difficulty would arise out of the plane "exceeding its maximum stability limits and encountering early morning turbulence caused by rising irregular currents of air. [In addition] the control, although hydraulically boosted, would be very stiff. Just the slightest control movements would have sent the airplane up or down at thousands of feet a minute."

> To propose that an alleged hijacker with limited experience could get a Boeing 767 lined up with a 208-foot-wide target and keep it lined up and hold his altitude at exactly 800 feet while being aurally bombarded with the clacker is beyond the realm of possibility... At the peak of my proficiency as a pilot, I know that I could not have done it on the first pass. And for two alleged hijackers, with limited experience to have hit the twin towers dead center on September 11, 2001, is total fiction. It could not happen."

Cell phone calls Are Impossible from Cruising Airliners

Central to the government's version are the cell phone calls that were supposedly made from cruising airliners on 9/11. From these calls, we learned that Muslim hijackers had taken control of the planes. Years later I learned that successful cell phone connections from cruising airliners were (practically) impossible in 2001 and were impossible as late as 2005 for the same technical reasons (and may also be to this day for the same reasons).

The reason cell phone calls from cruising airplanes were impossible in 2001 was because a cruising aircraft at 30,00 - 35,000 ft, traveling at 500 mph will pass beyond the range of the ground cellphone tower before the electronic connecting procedure, known as the "handshake" can be completed.

The speed of the airplane and the limitations of cellphone transmitting power of only five watts (usually only three) make cellphone communication unworkable from a cruising aircraft.[142] Cell phone power is deliberately limited to keep the costs of the phone down and to preserve battery life.

Experiments in the wake of 9/11 to determine the range of cell phones in airplanes have confirmed that the higher – and faster -- a plane travels – the fewer chances of success of a cell phone connection. Both Elias Davidsson and Mazzucco cite a well-known experiment conducted in Ontario, Canada, in 2003 by Prof A. K. Dewdney.[143] Dewdney found "a distinct trend of decreasing cell phone functionality with altitude" such that chances of success were less than one in a hundred for "a typical cell phone call from cruising altitude. (p. 218). Supporting such experimental findings, we learn that the basis of the business model of the airphone industry was to provide a service not available with cell phones.

When it became clear that claims that cell phone calls on 9/11 were problematic, supporters of the government version shifted their talking points to claim that the calls were made mostly on airphones. Mazzucco cites the example of U.S. Solicitor General, Ted Olson, who first claimed that his wife Barbara, a passenger on AA Flight 77, (Pentagon crash), called him with her cellphone. However, he later changed his story and claimed she made her calls on an airphone.

The difficulty for the airphone version is that there is official testimony from FBI interviews with the recipients of calls from the 9/11 passengers that the calls came from cell phones, not airphones in at least nine cases. Recipients of calls reported that they could tell from their caller IDs that the calls came from cell phones. This testimony was so definitive that the government and debunkers alike were forced to acknowledge that in two cases the calls were made from cell phones, with the implication perhaps that in these two cases, the odds were defied, and the cell phone calls were connected despite the technical challenges. Left unaddressed by official sources are the testimonies of at least seven other calls.

Both Mazzucco and Davidsson present a good deal of additional evidence that suggests that the phone calls did not take place on cruising airplanes. The record is rife with all sorts of inconsistencies and anomalies. Typically, there is no convincing airplane noise or sounds of struggle or panic, or credible witness testimony of what might be expected to happen in the case of a hijacking. In more than one instance the time of the phone call doesn't match up with the government scenario of when they were hijacked.

A notable example is the celebrated case of Todd Beamer, a passenger on UA 93, whose widely reported "Let's roll," battle cry, as reported by Lisa Jefferson, a GTA Airphone operator, decisively established, in the public mind, the scenario of the passenger uprising that supposedly caused his plane to crash near Shanksville, PA.

Mazzucco summarizes some of the anomalies in the record. According to the 9/11 Commission the hijacking took place at 9: 28. His call to Lisa Jefferson was connected at 9:43, but the contents of his call are strikingly at odds with the official narrative. Beamer stated that the plane was about to be hijacked by three individuals with knives including one with a bomb strapped to his waist. Jefferson estimated that the call lasted 7 minutes before the hijackers entered the cockpit.

This would have been at about 9:52, but according to the 9/11 Commission Report, the hijacking took place at 9:28. Mazzucco asks how Beamer could be describing events that are supposed to be happening in front of his eyes, when in fact they had already happened half an hour before. How could they be preparing to take control of the flight when they had already been in the cockpit for 15 minutes?

And this is only one of many anomalies that Davidsson records in his fifteen-page records of the details surrounding Todd Beamer's call. Davidsson opens his discussion of this call citing Blogger John Doe II's summary: "There is basically not a single sentence of the call that is not in dispute...Even the famous last words, "Let's Roll" are in dispute. (Davidsson, p. 185)

Calls Actually Came from Cell Phones

Since it's clear that cell phone calls were made and that they could not have been made from the air, the question becomes where and under what circumstances were they made?

Mazzucco's five-hour documentary includes a twenty-minute section analyzing this question (the last section of DVD 1,) with chapter headings such as "What happened to the passengers?" "The cell phone calls" and "If not from the planes, from where?"

What Happened to the Airplane Passengers on 9/11?

Mazzucco frankly admits that we are not likely to ever get the true story of what happened to the passengers, but from the available evidence he is able to suggest a not unlikely scenario wherein the government arranged for some sort of mid-air swap in order to confuse the air traffic control system. He explains that such a scheme would have been similar to the CIA plan proposed by the Joint Chiefs of Chief-of-Staff and rejected by President Kennedy in the 1960s. Codenamed Operation Northwoods, the plan called for the shoot-down and murder of airplane passengers to be attributed to Fidel Castro's government as a pretext for regime change.

The proposal "involved the in-flight swapping of commercial airliners with military drones." On 9/11, the airplanes could have been swapped "with a military drone in mid-air unbeknownst to the air traffic controllers. After the swap, the airliner[s] would be landed in a military base. The drone would continue to fly appearing on the radar as the original plane and would be remotely guided all the way into the target." The airline passengers would have been taken to a military base (or some other unknown location) and under the pretext of cooperating with a terror exercise, pressured into making the phone calls.

Perhaps the most striking bit of evidence that the phone calls were scripted and the callers under duress comes at the end of the voicemail left by flight attendant Cee Cee Lyles for her husband At the end of her cell phone call -- her mobile number was recorded on their caller ID -- she says goodbye to her family and whispers a clue at the very end.

Mazzucco gives the text of her revealing message. She begins by addressing her husband:

> Hi baby,
> I'm ...
> Baby, you have to listen to me carefully
> I'm on a plane that's been hijacked.
> I'm on the plane.
> I'm calling from the plane.
> I want to tell you I love you
> Please tell my children that I love them very much and I'm so
> sorry babe.
> (Mazzucco adds: we notice the absence of background noise.)
> I don't know what to say.
> There are three guys
> They've hijacked the plane
> I'm trying to be calm
> We're turned around and I've heard that there are planes that
> been, been flown into the World Trade Center.
> I hope to be able to see your face again baby.
> I love you.
> Goodbye,
> (Mazzucco: "After saying goodbye she seems to fumble with the
> headset as she whispers a few more words into the mouthpiece."
> It's a frame.

In his video, Mazzucco repeats her last whispered words, "It's a frame," several times. Most people I suppose will conclude that she intends a subversive message. Supporting the theory that the phone calls were scripted, Davidsson adds the intriguing detail that at the end of Cee Cee's call, some acute listeners claim to be able to hear someone whisper ... 'You did great." (p. 303)

Davidsson writes that if someone actually said that to her it would support the view "that she was acting within the framework of a hijacking drill." (p. 303) It's not difficult to imagine why Cee Cee Lyles's handler would have been pleased. She made two important points. She was witness to a hijacking, and she was clear that she feared for her life.

Zeus and Leda

Yeats's famous poem, "Leda and the Swan," begins with a rape, "a sudden blow" when Zeus, king of the gods, in the guise of a swan, a false flag, exploits his dominion to achieve his purpose. In Yeats's retelling of the myth, Zeus's rape leads step by step to the fall of Troy, to the end of civilization.

> The broken wall, the burning roof and tower
> And Agamemnon dead.

The 9/11 attacks were also a beginning: the beginning of a crusade, stoking permanent war, making the world a battlefield in accord with the vision of Dick Cheney, Donald Rumsfeld, and their neocon brethren.

Kevin Walsh's two-minute production, "Flight 175 – Slow Motion Video," in the minds of many viewers, puts the lie to one of the signature videos that helped propel the U.S. and the world into its "war on terror," its current tailspin.

Question: Do you have two minutes to look at a video?
CNN Flight 175 Slow Motion.mp4
<https://vimeo.com/562690141>

□

9/11, THE BETRAYAL OF AMERICA

By Elias Davidsson

2018

Editor's Notes

Elias Davidsson, an Icelandic activist, researcher and author, currently living in Germany, has written five books on the 9/11 and post – 9/11 terror attacks, including one each on the terror attacks of London 7/7 and the Mumbai, India, attacks of 2008. Davidsson's work is inspired by the anomalies in the official accounts of these episodes, pointing in each case to government-organized conspiracies, false flags everyone blaming radical Islamic terrorists, while shielding the actual perpetrators.

I have chosen excerpts from Davidsson's latest not yet published book on the terror events of 9/11, The Betrayal of America: Revisiting the 9/11 Evidence, focusing on the lack of evidence for hijackers and the absence of evidence of airliner crashes; specifically, the lack of credible evidence of the wreckage that should have resulted if four passenger planes had crashed on that day.

Davidsson undertook thorough original research on these incidents, searching out the details, and seeking information from specific airlines, the U.S. government, etc.

When I asked Davidsson via email, his views on the theory of no planes on 9/11, he agreed that there were no passenger plane crashes. He wrote that crashes of passenger planes on 9/11 "can safely be excluded" largely because of the "lack of evidence for such crashes." Similarly, he found that there was no credible evidence of hijackings or hijackers. These are "definite and unassailable facts."

As to what caused the apparent crashes, Davidsson wrote that he believed that it was likely that some airborne object (remotely controlled military aircraft, drone or missile) impacted the Twin Towers and the Pentagon," but that he was "open to other views." Similarly, he wrote that he is "convinced that no aircraft crashed at Shanksville, PA."

The primary purpose of his research, he explained, has been to determine whether 9/11 was an Islamic operation (involving Al Qaeda and Bin Laden). The conclusion, which he says he has held for ten years is that "9/11 was an operation led by the Pentagon whose main authors were Dick Cheney and Donald Rumsfeld. This is also the conclusion of many others."

In the excerpts below, I have made a few tiny emendations for clarity and likewise, for technical reasons, I have not included his footnotes. Davidsson's book contains nearly a thousand footnotes.

***

No Evidence of 19 Muslim Hijackers

(from *Betrayal of America*, Chapter 3)

The official account of 9/11 is based on a hijacking narrative according to which 19 individuals, whose names and photographs have been posted on the website of the FBI, *boarded* aircraft assigned to American Airlines flights 11 (AA11), and 77 (AA77), and United Airlines flights 175 (UA175) and 93 (UA93) on the morning of 11 September 2001.

These individuals are said to have then hijacked those aircraft in flight and crashed the aircraft in suicide attacks into three symbolic landmarks in the United States.

According to the official account, an aircraft assigned to flight AA11 was flown into the North Tower of the WTC in New York; shortly thereafter an aircraft assigned to flight UA175 was flown into the South Tower of the WTC. At 9:37 a.m. an aircraft assigned to flight AA77 impacted the Pentagon in Washington, D.C. The fourth aircraft, assigned to flight UA93, crashed in an empty field near Shanksville, Pennsylvania, after the passengers had risen up against the alleged hijackers and attempted to retake control of the aircraft. It was later surmised that the pilot of the aircraft had intended to crash into the White House.

Within hours of the operation, the FBI began to interview airline and airport employees who could provide information about what they had experienced that morning before and during the boarding of these flights. It must therefore be assumed that all relevant evidence about the boarding of the four aircraft has been obtained by the FBI.

-- Did the individuals designated by the US government as the hijackers of 9/11, board the designated flights?

-- Shortly after the FBI released the names and photographs of the alleged hijackers, questions about their identities began to emerge.

--The family of Hamza al-Ghamdi, one of the alleged hijackers, said the photo released by the FBI "has no resemblance to him at all."

-- CNN broadcast a picture of another alleged hijacker, identified as Saeed al-Ghamdi. That man, a pilot, was from Tunisia and was apparently still alive.

-- The photograph of a Saudi pilot by the name of Waleed al-Shehri was released by the FBI as one of the alleged hijackers: he protested his innocence from Casablanca, Morocco.

-- Two people with the name of Abdulaziz Alomari presented themselves, surprised to see their names on the FBI list of suspected hijackers. One of them, a Saudi engineer, said he lost his passport while studying in Denver, Colorado, in 1995. Of the FBI list, he said: "The name is my name, and the birth date is the same as mine. But I am not the one who bombed the World Trade Center in New York.

-- Another Abdulaziz Alomari was found working as a pilot with Saudi Airlines.

--Salem al-Hazmi, also listed by the FBI as an alleged hijacker, was indignant at being named as a suspect for mass murder. He said he worked in a petrochemical plant in Yanbu (Saudi Arabia).

-- Abdul Rahman al-Haznawi, brother of another suspect, said "There is no similarity between the photo published [on Thursday] and my brother." He said he did not believe his brother was involved in the crime: "He never had any such intention.

-- Gaafar al-Lagany, the Saudi government's chief spokesman in the United States, said that the hijackers probably stole the identities of legitimate Saudi pilots. These findings have been corroborated independently by Jay Kolar. The FBI disregarded these stories and maintained the names and photographs it originally posted on its website as those "believed to be the hijackers" of 9/11, including those of living individuals.

The 9/11 Commission (see Chapter 13) did not address these conflicting identifications. One basic goal of a criminal investigation is to identify the perpetrators. In order to prove that particular individuals could have hijacked an aircraft, it must be first demonstrated that they boarded that particular aircraft.

In order to demonstrate this fact, at least some of the following four classes of evidence should have been produced by the U.S. authorities in September 2001 or shortly thereafter:

1. Authenticated passenger lists (also called flight manifests), listing the names of all the passengers and crew members, including those suspected of hijacking.
2. Authenticated security videos from the airports, which depict the passengers (and the alleged hijackers).
3. Sworn testimonies of personnel who attended the boarding of the aircraft.
4. Formal identification of the bodily remains from the crash sites, accompanied by chain-of-custody reports.

The selection from *The Betrayal of America* below takes up evidence regarding the passenger lists. Davidsson believes that if the evidence of such lists does not exist or is "deemed to lack credibility, it is likely that these individuals did not board the aircraft and that, consequently, no "Islamic hijackings" had taken place."

No Authenticated Passenger Lists

The primary source used by airlines to identify the victims of aircraft crashes is the passenger list (sometimes designated as the flight manifest). A passenger list is a legal document proving – also for insurance purposes - those particular individuals boarded an aircraft. To ensure the reliability of passenger lists airlines check the identities of passengers who board the aircraft. In order to serve as legal documents, passenger lists must be duly authenticated by those responsible for their accuracy.

With regard to the four 9/11 flights, American and United Airlines have consistently refused to demonstrate that they possess authenticated passenger lists of these flights. Surprisingly, neither the corporate media nor the 9/11 Commission demanded the release of these authenticated documents.

FBI and Airlines' Refusal to Release Authentic Lists

In 2004 I attempted to obtain from American Airline's copies of authenticated passenger lists for the two American Airlines flights of 9/11. Karen Temmerman, Customer Relations, American Airlines, responded to me on 9 September 2004:

> At the time of the incidents, we released the actual passenger manifests to the appropriate government agencies who in turn released certain information to the media. These lists were published in many major periodicals and are now considered public records. At this time we are not in a position to release further information or to republish what the government agencies provided to the media.

The airline did not explain why it was not in a position to confirm what had already been for a long time in the public domain. On November 29, 2005, I tried again to obtain the passenger list of flight AA77 from American Airlines.

Sean Bentel of American Airlines first sent me a typed list that consisted of nothing more than the first and last names of 53 passengers from that flight. The list did not include Arab names. Asking again for "something more authentic," Sean Bentel responded that" the names I sent you are accurate... There may have been a formatting problem."

In turn, I responded that the problem was not the formatting of the data. Here is what I wrote:

> What I am asking is a replica of the original passenger list (either a scan of the original, or at least a document faithfully reflecting the contents of that list) ... [namely] the list of the paying passengers who boarded AA77. Can I take it that the list you sent me faithfully reflects the names of the paying passengers who boarded AA77?

Within hours Sean Bentel answered in the most laconic manner: "Mr. Davidsson, Names of terrorists were redacted. Sean Bentel."

Asked in return "[w]hy can't you send me a facsimile copy of the passenger lists, including the names of the terrorists," Sean Bental answered, "This is the information we have for public release." This was the end of this exchange.

I also turned to United Airlines. On October 21, 2004, I asked per email why the original flight manifests have not yet been publicized and whether United Airlines had provided some media with a copy of the original flight manifests.

The airline answered that "[a]ll matters pertaining to the September 11th terrorist attacks are under the investigation of the U.S. Federal Authorities. Please contact the FBI."

That was it. Numerous individuals have attempted without success to obtain authentic passenger lists from the airlines, among them Thomas R. Olmsted, M.D. He wrote, for example:

> I attempted on three occasions to obtain a final passenger list from American Airlines. They refuse to give a list and in fact, won't even verify that they gave the first list to CNN. Since the [unauthenticated] list is in the public domain, I find it curious that they would not take ownership nor provide a current, 'correct list'.

I did not give up. In February 2012, I requested on the basis of the Freedom Of Information Act (FOIA) from the FBI the release of Document 302, serial 7134, which contains "flight manifests for hijacked flights" and "information related to manifests." The request was denied.

As the names of all victims and alleged hijackers were publicized within days after 9/11, I could not fathom any plausible reason for the refusal of the airlines and the FBI to confirm the accuracy and authenticity of information that already exists in the public domain.

Authenticated passenger lists were neither provided to the Congressional Joint Inquiry of 2002 nor to the 9/11 Commission. It must therefore be presumed that no genuine passenger lists for the four 9/11 flights exist or that whatever the airlines and the FBI do possess does not correspond with the official allegations.

To sum up: No document has been produced by the airlines or the U.S. government proving that anyone, let alone the alleged terrorists, had boarded any of the four flights that were allegedly hijacked on 9/11.

No Validated Passenger Plane Wreckage Found (Implausible Crash Sites)

(from *Betrayal of America* Chapter 9)

Editor's Notes

In this section, Davidsson limits his discussion to whether the aircraft assigned to flights AA11, UA175, AA77 and UA93 crashed at the locations assigned by the official narrative. In the preceding chapter, it was shown that the FBI, the agency responsible for investigating the crime of 9/11, did not attempt to link the wreckage found at the reported crash sites to specific aircraft.

The evidence Davidsson produces is consistent with the likelihood that there were no passenger aircraft crashes on September 11, 2001. Davidsson's insistence in the selection below is limited to the "paucity or complete absence of physical evidence that would be expected after crashes of commercial airliners."

The Strange Crash Site at Ground Zero

The only official document containing photographs of debris attributed to the aircraft that allegedly crashed into the Twin Towers of the WTC is FEMA's WTC Building Performance Study (BPAT).

"Piece of Flight 11 gear"

"Piece of Flight 175 fuselage"

One photograph depicts an alleged "piece of Flight 11 landing gear" and one depicts an alleged "piece of Flight 175 fuselage." That is all. No known attempts were made by the FBI to forensically identify these parts.

The so-called photographic evidence, that is, these two photographs, do not permit the determination of the origin of the photographed objects, the type of aircraft to which they belonged, the aircraft's identity, or the circumstances that brought these objects to the location where they were photographed. It is inconceivable that these parts are all that remained from two Boeing 767-200 aircraft (flights AA11 and UA175), whose combined empty weight is 350,000 pounds. The dearth of photographed aircraft debris suggests that these two photographs do not depict debris from the Boeing 767-200 aircraft that allegedly crashed there.

According to the "Final Report of the 9/11 Commission," the four "black boxes" of the aircraft designated as belonging to flights AA11 and UA175 (two in each aircraft) were not found. This may appear plausible at first due to the complete destruction of the buildings. Yet Ted Lopatkiewicz, spokesman for the National Transportation Safety Board, said, "It's extremely rare that we don't get the recorders back. I can't recall another domestic case in which we did not recover the recorders."

The claim by the FBI that the "black boxes" were not found stretches credulity because numerous hard computer disks were reportedly found in the WTC rubble with information that could later be recovered. In addition, the rubble was later sifted in order to look for far smaller objects, including human nails and teeth.

Incredibly, as of the spring of 2002, no passenger remains from flights AA11 and UA175 had been found at Ground Zero.

The Strange Crash Site at the Pentagon

According to the official account, a Boeing 757 crashed into the Pentagon. Such an aircraft weighs well over 100,000 pounds. Dave McCowan, quoted by David Ray Griffin, notes that the debris found within the Pentagon represents at most one percent of that weight, thus raising the question what happened to 99% of the plane.

Lee Evey, the Pentagon Renovation Manager, said on 15 September 2001, however, that "[t]here are other parts of the plane that are scattered about outside the building. None of these parts are very large, however. You don't see big pieces of the airplane sitting there extending up into the air. But there are many small pieces. And the few larger pieces there look like they are veins out of the aircraft engine. They're circular."

It has not been explained why plane parts would be scattered outside the Pentagon. On 20 September 2001, a press conference was held by Assistant Director of the FBI's Washington Field Office Van Harp, Chief Ed Flynn of the Arlington County Police Department and Major General James Jackson of the Military District of Washington.

Asked by journalists about the wreckage of the plane that reportedly crashed at the Pentagon, Harp answered, "Well, at the outset, I should have stated, I cannot get into the details of the investigation nor the so-called crime scene." [Harp's first comment, days earlier, was an expression of bafflement that no significant plane wreckage was visible in the aftermath of the attack.] To a similar question, Harp answered, "All I can say is there has been some evidence already recovered with no more specificity." The reluctance of the FBI to provide even minimal information about the wreckage, even refusing to acknowledge the finding of the "black boxes," is surprising.

Photographic Evidence of Debris

At the trial of Zacarias Moussaoui [the alleged 20th hijacker], the following single blurred photograph was presented as evidence that a commercial aircraft had crashed into the Pentagon. This photograph is entitled "airplane parts in the Pentagon after Flight 77 crashed into the building." Zacarias Moussaoui was induced by the prosecution and by his defenders to confirm the authenticity of this photograph "without any further foundation."

Another photograph, circulated on the internet, purports to depict a fuselage piece from an American Airlines aircraft lying on the lawn outside the Pentagon. It is attributed to photographer Mark Faram, a long-time staff photographer of the Military Times. The photograph, presented below, has not been authenticated by
the FBI as belonging to a specific aircraft and was not presented as evidence at the Moussaoui trial.

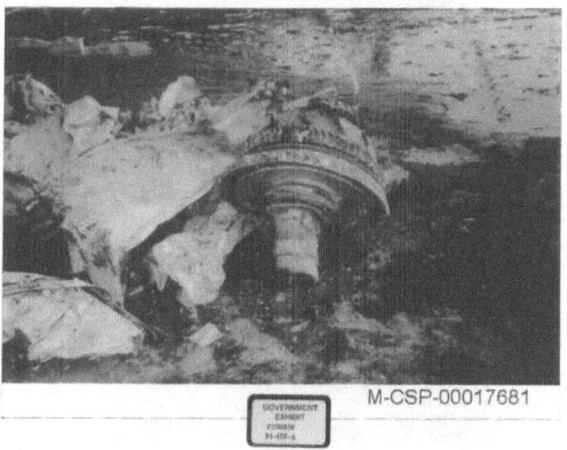

M-CSP-00017681

The evidence from the Pentagon crash site suggests, nevertheless, that some airborne object may have crashed at the Pentagon but does not permit us to determine the type of object, its identity and the exact circumstances that led that object into the building.
Captain Daniel Davis, former U.S. Army Air Defense Officer and NORAD Tac Director, as well as the founder and former CEO of Turbine Technology Services Corp., made the following statement:

"As a former General Electric Turbine engineering specialist and manager and then CEO of a turbine engineering company, I can guarantee that none of the high-tech, high-temperature alloy engines on any of the four planes that crashed on 9/11 would be completely destroyed, burned, shattered or melted in any crash or fire. Wrecked, yes, but not destroyed. Where are all those engines, particularly at the Pentagon? If jet-powered aircraft crashed on 9/11, those engines, plus wings and tail assembly, would be there."

Here is a photograph of a Boeing 757 engine. Each such aircraft carries two huge engines.

Barry and son, Brian in front of a B-757 engine on the occasion of his retirement flight, June 21, 1998 (Karlene Petitt)

It stretches credulity that both of these engines were "vaporized" in the crash and that the contents of the cockpit voice recorder (CVR) were destroyed "by the intense heat it had been subjected to," while the bodily remains of virtually all those who died there could be identified, and, most incredibly of all, two pieces of a Virginia Driver's License were reportedly recovered from the site bearing the following readable information about one of the alleged hijackers:

> Name: Majed M GH Moqed Address: 5913 Leesburg Pike, Apartment #08 Falls Church, Virginia 22041-2210 Customer Number: A69-60-0405; Height: 5'7"

Was this driver's license made out of steel more fire-resistant than the two Boeing engines?

Video Footage of An Aircraft Impact

The Pentagon is surrounded by dozens of security cameras, but the Department of Defense has not been able (or willing) to produce credible footage that would document the approaching airborne object. The single video sequence released by the Pentagon after much prodding does not show anything resembling an aircraft. Below are the two first frames of this sequence. The experts who created these stills claimed that due to a software bug, the computer stamped the date and time when the stills were extracted from the footage rather than the actual time of impact.

Sep. 12, 2001, 17:37:19   plane

Sep. 12, 2001, 17:37:19   impact

FBI Special Agent Jacqueline Maguire declared in a court statement made under penalty of perjury that she was tasked by her supervisor "to determine whether the FBI possessed any videotapes that may have captured the impact of Flight 77 into the Pentagon on September 11, 2001." She stated that the above sequence "shows Flight 77 hitting the Pentagon" and that this footage "would be used as evidence in the case of U.S. v. Zacarias Moussaoui."

Asked whether this was the only footage "concerning Flight 77 in the possession of the FBI," she responded that "although the FBI possessed other videotapes that depicted the Pentagon on September 11, 2001, those videotapes depicted only post-impact scenes, and therefore, did not show the impact of Flight 77 into the Pentagon."

Note that Maguire did not refer only to footage made by the Pentagon closed-circuit security cameras but generally to "videotapes," a designation that may include footage made by reporters. Indeed, she said that the other videotapes depicted only "post-impact scenes," which evidently did not originate from security cameras.

On 9 November 2006, Brian Austin and Steve Pennington were interviewed by Diane Putney in the Office of the Secretary of Defense in Arlington, Virginia.

These two men were responsible for the operation of the security cameras of the Pentagon. Brian Austin said he was employed by Radeon Corporation. His employer at the time of the attacks was Radian Inc., which in 2006 became DRS Radian. None of these companies could be located.

Austin's job, he said, was to keep the cameras, the AMAG security system, and the Loronix video recording system in working order. When the Pentagon event on 9/11 occurred, Austin said he was located at the PFPA (The Pentagon police department) at Federal Office Building 2, across the street from the Pentagon. He said he and colleagues were doing maintenance work, but "can't elaborate exactly."

Steve Pennington said to the interviewer that he is one of the two partners that own Chesapeake Marketing Associates. That company is actually called Chesapeake & Midlantic Marketing, in short MIDCHES. The company is located in Abingdon, Maryland. He said he was acting "more or less" as a consultant to Radeon [sic] and the Pentagon Force Protection people, "mainly for security cameras and some of the infrastructure for some of their systems...We design the connectivity of the systems."

Pennington said that two security cameras captured the approaching aircraft. One of these is on YouTube captioned "Pentagon 9/11 Plane Crash Video 1." It does not allow a determination of the nature of the object that appears to approach the Pentagon. Pennington told the interviewer that he was the person who created the famous stills of an "approaching aircraft" shown in these pages, which display the wrong date and time. He said:

> [T]he system records the date and time, and we actually searched the event by date and time when we were looking at the event and capturing information.

Unfortunately, the software had a bug in it and when a still image was saved it captured the time on the computer at the time you were capturing the image or saving the image from the video to becoming a still picture...That has long since been corrected, but that is the reason that the time and date are wrong.

Assuming that the aforementioned software bug could not be corrected at the time, that stills from a video could not have been taken by different means and that the FBI did not mind disseminating stills with the wrong date and time, what explains the lack of a date and time on the video clip that was released? Was there a second bug? And if so, how could Pennington search the event "by date and time"?

Asked about the unusually slow rate of the recording, Pennington said that "at that time they were being recorded at one image per second, [because] the system was a new system and wasn't even government property. It was installed at the facility, but it had not yet been tested and turned over. That's why the images were being captured at a lower-than-normal rate."

Pennington furthermore revealed that due to renovation, many or most security cameras on that side of the Pentagon were inoperative. Other cameras would normally look at that area, but because that area was being renovated, a lot of the connectivity of these cameras and the infrastructure that allowed those cameras to be connected back to the building had been removed or destroyed, so they weren't capturing images and offering fields of view," he said. In fact, "every camera on that side of the building was disconnected during the construction project and it was purely happenstance that the system happened to be running because it wasn't supposed to be running for another month.

According to the above account, those responsible for security at the Pentagon authorized the disconnection of video surveillance of that side of the building for an entire month. Since this episode at the Pentagon, the dysfunction of surveillance cameras has become a regular pattern when terrorists are at work. This happened during the London attacks of 7 July 2005, during the Mumbai attacks of 26 November 2008 and in other terrorist attacks. This mysterious phenomenon begs for a scientific explanation.

In sum, there is no reliable visual evidence that an aircraft, a missile, or anything at all crashed into the Pentagon. If it was an aircraft, it is not clear what aircraft it was. And to crown all these questions, it is not even clear when the event occurred.

The Strange Crash Site at Somerset County, PA

No Visible Aircraft Wreckage

Many of those who rushed to the reported crash site of flight UA93 at Somerset County near Shanksville, were surprised to see no plane wreckage, nothing but a hole in the ground. Here are a series of observations from local people and journalists who arrived at the scene shortly after what they were told was a plane crash:

-- Mark Stahl of Somerset, a salesman, arrived at the site 15 minutes after an explosion. He told the *Tribune-Review* that he didn't realize a passenger jet had crashed until a firefighter told him. "It's unbelievable," he said. To CNN he said, "the plane is pretty much disintegrated. There's nothing left but scorched trees." Yet, on 12 September 2001, the *Wall Street Journal* claimed that Mark had "snapped pictures of the downed plane [and] showed color photos of wreckage surrounded by a crater and flames." No one apparently has ever seen these pictures.

-- Homer Barron, a worker at Stoystown Auto Wreckers, told the *Pittsburgh Post-Gazette* that he and his coworker, Jeff Phillips, drove to the "crash scene" and found there a smoky hole in the ground: "It didn't look like a plane crash because there was nothing that looked like a plane," he said. His colleague, however, said, "There was one part of a seat burning up there. That was something you could recognize."

-- Scott Spangler, a photographer with a local newspaper, was quoted in the book *Running Toward Danger: Stories Behind the Breaking News of 9/11*: "I didn't think I was in the right place. I was looking for a wing or a tail. There was nothing, just this pit... I was looking for anything that said tail, wing, plane, metal. There was nothing."

--Frank Monaco of the Pennsylvania State Police commented, "If you would go down there, it would look like a trash heap. There's nothing but tiny pieces of debris. It's just littered with small pieces."

-- Jon Meyer, a reporter with WJAC-TV, said, "I was able to get right up to the edge of the crater... All I saw was a crater filled with small, charred plane parts. Nothing that would even tell you that it was the plane... There were no suitcases, no recognizable plane parts, no body parts. The crater was about 30 to 35 feet deep."

-- Ron Delano, a local who rushed to the scene after hearing about the crash, said, "If they hadn't told us a plane had wrecked, you wouldn't have known. It looked like it hit and disintegrated.

-- Gabrielle DeRose, a news anchor with KDKA-TV, viewed the crash site from a hill overlooking it and said, "It was very disturbing to think all the remains just disintegrated... There were no large pieces of airplane, no human remains, no baggage."

-- Rick King, a local assistant volunteer fire chief, who saw the crater at the crash site, said, "Never in my wildest dreams did I think half the plane was down there." King sent his men into the woods to search for the plane's fuselage, but they kept coming back, telling him, "Rick. There's nothing."

-- Wells Morrison, a local FBI agent, told author Glenn Kashurba that after arriving at the crash site his first thought was, "Where is the plane?" because "what I saw was this honeycomb looking stuff, which I believe is insulation or something like that. I was not seeing anything that was distinguishable either as human remains or aircraft debris."

-- Faye Hahn, an emergency medical technician (EMT), who arrived at the crash site, stated: "Several trees were burned badly and there were papers everywhere. We searched...I was told that there were 224 passengers, but later found out that there were actually forty. I was stunned. There was nothing there."

-- Joe Little, a 10 News reporter was working less than four miles from the crash site on the morning of 9/11 for an ABC/FOX affiliate. He said he and a photographer arrived on the crash scene within 30 minutes and were able to walk right up to the crater. He said there was nothing there other than a crater, some smoke and a few charred trees. In a report he filed he wrote: "I still can't see a fire let alone a plane."

-- Nina Lensbouer, the wife of a local former volunteer firefighter, told the *Pittsburgh Post-Gazette*, that after seeing a mushroom flame rising, her first instinct was to run toward it, to try to help. "But I got there and there was nothing, nothing there but charcoal. Instantly, it was charcoal."

-- Thomas Spallone, a state police spokesman, said "everything just disintegrated. There are just shreds of metal. The longest piece I saw was 2 feet long."

-- Nick Tweardy of Stonycreek Township, who came to help with the rescue effort said "You couldn't see nothing. We couldn't tell what we were looking at. There's just a huge crater in the woods."

-- Brad Reiman, a young man from Berlin in Somerset County, said "the tail was a short distance from the rest of the wreckage. It looked like the plane hit once and flopped down into the woods." The largest piece of wreckage he could identify looked like a section of the plane's tail, he said.

No one else, apparently, saw this tail section. On 13 September 2001, the *Pittsburgh Post-Gazette* reported that a self-piloting helicopter developed by Carnegie Mellon University's Robotics Institute was sent to Somerset County to photograph the scene. According to the *Post-Gazette*, the 14-foot-long helicopter "can quickly produce a highly detailed, three-dimensional map of the impact crater and the surrounding spread of debris." Chuck Torpe, director of the Robotics Institute was cited by the newspaper saying that the "aerial map can include objects as small as one or two inches in diameter." Pennsylvania Attorney General Mike Fisher said: "The aerial map may help identify key evidence faster than it might be found by physically canvassing the area." Where is that aerial map?

The Legend of The Buried Aircraft

The absence of visible debris led some reporters to conjecture that the plane did not disintegrate, but that the 155-foot-long fuselage had completely vanished into the spongy ground and was buried deep in the crater, hidden from view. Thus, Tom Gibb of the *Post-Gazette* speculated on 15 October 2001 that the "fuselage disintegrated in a crater that collapsed on itself."

This story reappeared in force a year after 9/11 and remained the official explanation for the lack of debris. Robb Frederick of *Tribune-Review* purported to know how it all happened. He wrote on 11 September 2002: "The plane pitched, then rolled, belly up. It hit nose-first, like a lawn dart...digging more than 30 feet into the earth, which was spongy from the old mine work."

The Australian paper, *The Age,* wrote that the "rest of the 757 continued its downward passage, the sandy loam closing behind it like the door of a tomb."

Wes Allison of the *St. Petersburg Times* wrote on 10 September 2003 that "the site had been mined for coal, then refilled with dirt. It was still soft when flight 93 crashed, and firefighters said the Boeing 757 tunneled right in. They had to dig 15 feet to find it."

Mary Jo Dangel of the *St. Anthony Messenger Online* explained in 2006 why the wreckage was not visible: "The ground had swallowed up much of the wreckage."

State police Major Frank Monaco from New Kensington told the *Post-Gazette* in 2006 that the plane had "burrowed into the soft, reclaimed earth of the former strip mine and crumpled like an accordion."

According to WTAE-TV, Pittsburgh, of 14 September 2001, citing FBI spokeswoman Linda Vizi, the cockpit voice recorder (CVR) from the aircraft assigned to flight UA93 was found "about 25 feet within the crater" at 8:25 p.m. on that day.

No independent observer was present, however, during the excavation. Blogger Killtown compiled an archive of reports that included the claim that most of the aircraft assigned to flight UA93 had been buried in the ground.

This compilation includes only a few eyewitness testimonies in support of that claim and are either couched in passive language or attributed to unnamed sources. Killtown then made the following very perceptive observation: "[T]here is absolutely no logical reason for the news not to have reported right away that most of the 155 ft-long, 60-ton [sic] Boeing 757 was found.

Contents of the plane that would have been found down in the ground along with the black boxes and engine that were reported would be: 44 passengers, their luggage, hundreds of passenger seats, 3 huge landing gears, 10 huge tires and rim, and possibly sections of the tail (since both black boxes located in the tail section supposedly burrowed far underground and there is no evidence of the tail section above ground), among tons and tons of other plane debris."
No such reports exist, so we may wonder, like Blogger "Dave," at the seemingly miraculous nature of the flight UA93 crash:

> As we all know, 11 September 2001 was "the day that everything changed." Enormous office buildings, for example, suddenly and inexplicably acquired the ability to drop into their own footprints with no assistance from demolition experts. Five-story masonry buildings [the Pentagon] suddenly acquired the extraordinary ability to swallow enormous airliners without leaving behind an appropriate entry hole or any trace of aircraft wreckage. And now we find, perhaps most amazingly of all, that the ground itself somehow also acquired the ability to swallow commercial aircraft. On that fateful day, and only on that day, a 100+ ton [sic] airplane measuring 155 feet long, 125 feet wide and 45 feet tall disappeared into a crater measuring, at most, "about 30 to 40 feet long, 15 to 20 feet wide and 18 feet deep." Any skilled magician, I suppose, could make an airplane disappear into a building. But making an entire airplane disappear without a trace in an empty field? I have to admit that that is pretty impressive.

Is it physically possible that a Boeing 757 could disappear totally into the ground when crashing, at any speed whatsoever? A comparison with a similar aircraft crash, that of Helios Airways flight 522, suggests an answer. That aircraft, a Boeing 737-300, hit a mountain in Greece on 14 August 2005 and plunged to the ground from an altitude of 34,000 feet. Yet the following photograph from that crash site shows that a large part of the tail section remained recognizable. Nothing similar was seen at the crash site of flight UA93.

The Invisible Recovery of The Wreckage

Despite the apparent absence of wreckage from an aircraft, as reported by witnesses, FBI agent Bill Crowley announced on 24 September 2001 - merely 13 days after 9/11 - that "95 percent of the plane was recovered...and the pieces of United Airlines Flight 93 that had been recovered were turned over Sunday to the airline..." He said that the biggest piece recovered was a 6 by-7-foot piece of the fuselage skin, including four windows. The heaviest piece, he said, was part of an engine fan, weighing about 1,000 pounds.

None of the eyewitnesses had mentioned having observed these objects at the crash site. With the exception of the two black boxes, all wreckage was reportedly passed on to United Airlines. Asked what United Airlines would do with the wreckage, an airline spokeswoman said, "I don't think a decision has been made... but we're not commenting." According to Jeff Plantz, senior investigator of flight safety at United Airlines, eight of the dumpsters that "contain the wreckage of United Flight 93 ... are currently [May 31, 2002] in a hangar in Somerset, Pennsylvania... The wreckage is the property of United Airlines' insurance company."

Although the FBI ended its reported recovery work, the site remained surrounded by a chain-link fence. Wallace Miller warned: "If anybody is caught penetrating that perimeter and disregarding [the no-trespassing] signs, they will be prosecuted to the fullest extent of the law."

Michael Renz of the German public television station ZDF tried to film the wreckage of the aircraft that allegedly crashed at Somerset County for a documentary. After asking for permission from United Airlines, he and his team were told that an insurance company had custody of the wreckage. The insurance company said it could not provide any information: The responsible individual was in a meeting, then on a three-day business trip, then on the intercontinental trip that would take weeks. During this time he could not be reached by email or cell phone, or "so we were told by the secretary of one of the largest airline-insurance companies in the United States."

After weeks and countless phone calls, a brief answer came: "We do not have the wreckage. The FBI in Washington is in charge." The FBI press officer refused an interview but said he would certainly give permission to film the wreckage, though not immediately. But alas! The FBI no longer had the wreckage.

It has been returned to United Airlines. Back to square one! The producer returned to Germany without any evidence of the wreckage. The film producer described similar difficulties when he tried to obtain permission to film inside a Boeing flight simulator or when he approached New York officials to ask them about the fireproofing in the WTC. "But when we talk with officials off-the-record, many say a gag order has been handed from the top."

In 2006, after the trial of Zacarias Moussaoui, the U.S. Government released a set of photographs purporting to depict items found at the Pennsylvania crash site. These mostly low-quality photographs do not permit us to determine whether they relate to a Boeing 757, or whether they were found at the alleged crash site. In addition, no chain-of-custody reports accompanied these photographs.

Extreme Secrecy Surrounding the Crash Site

According to the *Tribune-Review*, the authorities "cordoned off the area within a 4-mile radius of the crash site" within hours after the incident. Later the FBI and state police confirmed that they had cordoned off a second area about six to eight miles away from the crater, where further debris were found.

On 13 September 2001, State Police Lieutenant Colonel Robert Hickes said that 280 state troopers were protecting the site. Using horses and helicopters, state police created a double ring of security around the area, spanning several miles. John M. Eller, police chief in Brookhaven, Pennsylvania, reported that approximately 600 troopers were utilized at the site in Shanksville, including 16 mounted troopers. In order to prevent unauthorized people from seeing the site, "inside and outside perimeters were established" and "checkpoints were established along ... roadways" leading to the site.

Initially, "the news media were staged in an area around the outer perimeter… The Major instructed that the news media be transported to the crash site in two buses.

They were permitted to photograph the site for one half-hour and then returned to the staging area." Paul Falavolito was working as a paramedic in Pittsburgh and followed the events of 9/11 as part of an on-site medical support team for rescue workers and family members who traveled to the Shanksville site.

Among his impressions:

Upon arrival at the site, we are greeted by a barrier of state police cars on a rural road in this town… At the checkpoint, we show our IDs and are allowed through. For the next two miles, I cannot believe my eyes. Down this country road, police cars and troopers are everywhere. Horseback troopers are patrolling the area… Checkpoints are everywhere… This is a scary feeling: I feel like I am in another country.

> The FBI strictly prevented journalists and members of the public from photographing the site. As an example, a township supervisor from Blair County by the name of Terence Claar was physically subdued by state troopers for trying to sneak into the site. As a result, he was hospitalized. He was the seventh person charged with trying to enter what was designated as a crime scene.

As a result of this secrecy, no photographs are available showing the recovery of the aircraft's wreckage. Few photos exist of the operations around the site. Among those is the following photograph showing a Penn State Police Mobile Command Post "during operation at the crash site of Flight 93 in Shanksville."

Were Personal Items Planted at The Crash Site?

As mentioned previously, eyewitnesses who came immediately to the site did not see anything there that suggested the wreckage of an aircraft. Yet the FBI claimed later to have found there an amazing collection of recognizable personal items that belonged to passengers,

crew members and alleged hijackers, some of them in good condition.

According to the FBI, the following items were recovered from the alleged crash site of flight UA 93 at Somerset County:

• Kingdom of Saudi Arabia ID card of alleged hijacker Ahmed Alnami (item Q1) • Saudi Arabian Youth Hostels Association ID Card for same (item Q2) • Three small color photographs, two strips of negatives and an enlarged photocopy of Kingdom of Saudi Arabia ID Card (items Q3) • Handwritten letter with possible Arabic writing (item Q45) • A "five page Arabic document [with] details regarding the strategy and preparation required to conduct a hijacking."

• Personal effects belonging to passengers Christian Adams, Lorraine Bay, Todd Beamer, Alan Beaven, Mark Bingham, Deora Bodley, Sandra Bradshaw, Marion Britton, Thomas Burnett, Bill Cashman, Georgine Corrigan, Patricia Cushing, Donald Greene, Linda Grondlund, Richard Guadagno, Jason Dahl, Patrick Driscoll, Edward Felt, Jane Folger, Colleen Fraser, Andrew Garcia, Jeremy Glick, Louis Nacke, Nicole Miller, John Talignani and Leroy Homer.

Another FBI document, released among the 9/11 Commission's papers in 2009, lists, in addition, the following knives or knife parts found at the site:
-- Q17 Black knife handle (your item #2)
-- Q18 Silver colored blade and piece of the black handle (your item #3)

-- Q44 Possible handmade knife (your item #20)
-- Q362 Pocket knife (Item 7, 1B26, Barcode E01991643)
--Q363 Multi-purpose utility tool with knife blade exposed (Item 29, 1B286, Barcode E01991317)
--Q377 Pocket knife (1B675, Barcode E01991305) Q380
[Several more such items are listed.]

The above FBI documents do not mention CeeCee Lyles' driving license, the passport of alleged hijacker Al Ghamdi,501 alleged hijacker Alnami's Florida Driver's License and a visa page from alleged hijacker Ziad Jarrah's passport, all of which were also allegedly found at the site.

Jerry and Beatrice Guadagno of Ewing, New Jersey, the parents of Richard Guadagno, a passenger aboard flight UA93, received Richard's credentials and his badge from the U.S. Fish and Wildlife Service that were reportedly found at the Shanksville site. Richard's sister Lori said of the credentials, which were returned in their wallet: "It was practically intact. It just looked like it wasn't damaged or hadn't gone through much of anything at all, which is so bizarre and ironic." Apart from some expressions of surprise by families who received intact personal effects - such as those of the Guadagnos - no one seemed to raise the question of how these items could be found in good condition while their owners did not leave a trace.
Planting aircraft parts, in order to fake a crash site, was actually envisaged by the U.S. military as part of Operation Northwoods (discussed in chapter 10):

> It is possible to create an incident that will make it appear that Communist Cuban MIGs have destroyed a USAF aircraft over international waters in an unprovoked attack...At precisely the same time that the aircraft was presumably shot down, a submarine or small surface craft would disburse F-101 parts, parachute, etc., at approximately 15 to 20 miles off the Cuban coast and depart.

> The pilots returning to Homestead would have a true story as far as they knew. Search ships and aircraft could be dispatched, and parts of aircraft found.

This plan, seriously considered by the U.S. military, demonstrates that planting incriminating evidence to fake an aircraft crash has been previously considered by U.S. public officials in support of what they regarded as overriding foreign policy objectives. The nature, number and condition of the items found at the alleged crash site of flight UA93 - as reported above - especially in the light of Operation Northwoods, support the view that the aforementioned personal items could have been planted to fake the crash of flight UA93.

Concluding Observations About the Somerset County Crash Site

The alleged crash site in Somerset County and the events that occurred there on the morning of 9/11 remain a mystery that the U.S. authorities clearly do not wish to reveal. Did an aircraft crash there at all? Was the site prepared in advance? Was a bomb detonated there to fake a crash? Were body parts actually found, and how were they identified? How can we reconcile the contradictions between the testimony of the local eyewitness and the official account? These questions need to be answered.

How did the 9/11 Commission address the testimony of eyewitnesses? It simply ignored them. This site is mentioned only a few times in the 9/11 Commission's Final Report and mainly to emphasize two points: that "no evidence of firearms or of their identifiable remains was found at the aircraft's crash site" and that "[t]he FBI collected 14 knives or portions of knives at the Flight 93 crash site."510

None of the eyewitnesses from Shanksville, whose testimony might have undermined the official account, was invited to testify before the 9/11 Commission. The Commission did not demand from the FBI any hard evidence proving that flight UA93 crashed at Shanksville.

Conclusions to Chapter 9

The main findings of this chapter are:

• Photographic evidence of aircraft wreckage from the three alleged crash sites is sparse and inconclusive.

• At none of the three locations designated as aircraft crash sites did eyewitnesses observe wreckage that could plausibly come from a Boeing 757 or 767 aircraft.

• No bodies or blood were sighted at the UA93 crash site, but numerous paper documents belonging to flight UA93 passengers and crew members were reportedly found there. □

DID DICK CHENEY PLAN TO ASSASSINATE PRESIDENT BUSH ON 9/11?

By Ronald Bleier

July 2019

B

y 10:03 a.m. on the morning of September 11, when UA Flight 93 purportedly crashed into a field near Shanksville, PA, we saw all the terror that we were going to see. Nevertheless, it took many hours and well into the day for the situation to calm down and for the nation to sense that things were more or less under control. Even so, it took three days for the U.S. to allow normal resumption of civil aviation and land travel. For many hours after 10 a.m., there was much confusion.

For example, as researcher Gerard Holmgren discovered, at various times, both American Airlines (AA) 77 and AA 11 reportedly struck New York City's World Trade Center (WTC). In the end, AA 77 was switched to the strike on the Pentagon. Regarding AA 77 in particular there were "wild discrepancies." First, it was reported that it had struck the WTC; then that it didn't even take off for a half hour after the second WTC strike. Later it was reported to have taken off at 9:33 a.m., but it somehow "flew 700 miles out to Ohio and back in just 5 minutes, to hit the Pentagon."

Holmgren also found from the U.S. Bureau of Transportation Statistics (BTS) that both these flights were "fictitious." Neither AA 77 nor AA 11 was scheduled to fly on 9/11, and neither did. Why didn't the terror planners simply revise these anomalous statistics either beforehand or shortly after 9/11 when the discrepancies would not have been discovered? Was it a simple oversight? Was it simply the arrogance of government planners who couldn't be bothered with such minute detail?

In any case, even after Holmgren published his discovery, it took years for the BTS data to be revised to conform to the official account.

Unlike the two American Airlines flights which never flew that day, the two other planes, both United Airlines (UA 175, N612; South Tower) and UA 93 (N591; Shanksville, PA) were actually scheduled and were airborne. But according to BTS records, Holmgren found, they did not crash on 9/11 since they were not destroyed until 2005.

Was President Bush A Target?

It was not until late on September 11th that concerns regarding the possibility of more terror attacks abated. In the course of the day, United Airlines reported that it took hours to sort the many false reports it received of hijackings, explosions, and other terror threats. For all the public knew there might have been more to come. Perhaps the plotters might have had in mind a menu of even more terror options. Perhaps they made on-the-spot decisions and in the end, limited the terror to what actually happened, or what the official narrative claims happened on 911.

I was reminded of the possibility that more terror might have been planned when I learned from Daniel Hopsicker's *Terrorland: Mohammed Atta and the 9/11 Cover-up,* (2004), that there had actually been an assassination attempt on the life of President Bush. It took determined reporting by Hopsicker to search out this information since the government made a point of suppressing news of the foiled attack. Hopsicker tracked down early press reports in the local media in Florida, acting, he writes, on a friend's "cynical dictum" that the most reliable information one gets in the wake of such high-profile events are these early press reports, untainted by the subsequent cover-up. (Hopsicker, p.40)

Shay Sullivan, reporting for the *Longboat Observer* of Sarasota, Florida, found a chance witness, Longboat Key Fire Marshall, Carroll Mooneyhan, who noted unusual activity at the president's hotel. Mooneyhan happened to be waiting at the front desk of the Colony Beach Resort at Longboat Key, at 6 a.m. when four Arab men in a white van arrived at the hotel's guard gate. They said they were scheduled for a morning "poolside interview" with the president. According to Mooneyhan, they even asked for a secret serviceman by name. The men were told to contact the president's public-relations office in Washington and were turned away. (Hopsicker, pp.44-45)

Two days earlier, on September 9, 2001, the popular Afghani Northern Alliance leader, Shad Massoud, was assassinated in Afghanistan with a disturbingly similar modus operandi. Two suicide bombers, posing as journalists had requested an interview with Massoud and set off a bomb hidden inside their television camera.

The Northern Alliance declared that Massoud's assassination was the work of Pakistan's intelligence agency, the ISI, which had close links to the CIA. Author David Ray Griffin cites author Michel Chossudovsky, who claims that the U.S. had been trying to weaken Massoud because he was a nationalist who had unified much of his region, and would very likely have balked at the U.S. plans to invade Afghanistan. After Massoud's death, the Northern Alliance became fragmented and significantly weaker, unable to contest U.S. war plans. (David Ray Griffin, *The New Pearl Harbor*, 2004, p.110)

News of what seems to be an attempt on the life of George W. Bush was firmly suppressed by U.S. officials. Witness Mooneyhan, who at first spoke freely to the *Longboat Observer*, was soon warned off. He said that after 9/11 he had been visited by the CIA and the Secret Service and he told Hopsicker that he preferred not to talk about what he witnessed because of concern for his career. He said he has to "be careful what he says." (Hopsicker, p. 48).

As to the four Arab men who turned out to be Sudanese, the AP reported that they were interrogated and soon released when no connection could be made to the 9/11 attacks. Similarly, the FBI "pooh-poohed" the apparent assassination attempt and the story got virtually no attention in the major media. (Hopsicker, p. 43)

The incident raises many obvious questions. Why were the four Arab men released? How did they know the whereabouts and the schedule of President Bush? How did they learn the name of a Secret Service agent? What connections, if any, did the Sudanese men have with U.S. intelligence agencies? Why was news of their attempt to interview President Bush suppressed and key witnesses warned of the story? One enormous red flag is that the circumstantial evidence of a connection between the Arabs and the U.S. security services is strong.

President Bush's Movements on 9/11

At about 8:30 a.m. President Bush traveled in a motorcade from his hotel to his scheduled photo-op at the Emma E. Booker Elementary School in Sarasota, Florida. On his way, after 8:46 a.m., he learned of an incident in NYC involving a strange plane crash into the North World Trade Center Tower. Soon after he took his place in a second-grade classroom and watched and participated in a reading lesson about a pet goat. At 9:03 a.m. he was told in a whisper by Andy Card, his chief of staff that "America is under attack."[144]

Instead of briskly responding to the emergency, as might be expected of a commander-in-chief, he remained calm, if not repressed, as if he were following a script. (In one video I saw years ago -- apparently no longer available on the internet -- I detected a moment when Bush's lips parted into a brief smirk before they darted back into a tight line).

Evidently, when the conspirators set up Bush's Florida photo-op, they correctly assumed that the public would not learn, at least in a timely way, of the irresponsible manner in which President Bush responded to the emergency.

(Perhaps the main lesson this incident emphasizes is that in such false flag operations, timeliness is all. Had the video been available in the days following 9/11, pointed questions might have been asked, and U.S. foreign and domestic policy substantially altered.) Nevertheless, the conspirators were undoubtedly later embarrassed by the wide release of Moore's documentary.

Instead of reacting quickly to the news of the shock and awe of the ongoing terror in New York City, and immediately taking up his role as chief executive of the United States, President Bush spent perhaps the next 10 minutes or so after 9:03 a.m. calmly listening to children read and, every so often, making his own cringe-worthy contributions to the lesson. Even after he left the classroom, he lingered at the school, talking with students and teachers and posing for photos. During this period, neither he nor members of his entourage, including his security detail, showed any special concern for their own safety, not to mention national security. The one exception was an anonymous Marine who, when he heard the news of the second attack at the WTC, said to the local sheriff, "We're out of here. Can you get everyone ready?" He was overruled.

Not until 9:35 a.m. did Bush's motorcade move out to the Sarasota airport where Air Force One was waiting. Finally, at 9:55 a.m., Bush and his entourage were airborne, "incredibly" – as the authors of the History Commons put it, -- without fighter protection. This unexplained lapse in security is yet another example consistent with the president's evident intention to leave the direction of U.S. policy to his vice president. It was only after he was airborne that he began his struggle with Dick Cheney to take charge of his movements.

At Booker Elementary, Bush gave people to understand that he intended an immediate return to Washington. But soon after takeoff Bush, Cheney and the Secret Service "began arguing whether it was safe to fly back to the capital" due to proliferating terror threats. Bush's Chief of Staff, Andrew Card advised caution: "We've got to let the dust settle before we go back."

At the time, there were still over 3,000 planes in the air over the US [USA Today, 8/13/02 (B)], including about half of the planes in the region of Florida where Bush was. [St. Petersburg Times, 9/7/02] Recall, too, that the Secret Service learned of a threat to Bush and Air Force One "just minutes after Bush left Booker Elementary." Karl Rove, also on Air Force One, confirmed that a dangerous threat was known before the plane took off: "They also made it clear they wanted to get us up quickly, and they wanted to get us to a high altitude because there had been a specific threat made to Air Force One … A declaration that Air Force One was a target and said in a way that they called it credible.

Assuming that both Cheney and Bush knew that reports of threats **from foreign entities** to Air Force One (and to the rest of the country) were bogus, it's not surprising that Bush was not a happy camper. For the next half-hour, before he bowed to Cheney's "advice," Air Force One simply circled the Sarasota airport, while Bush fought for an immediate return to the White House. But Cheney won. After their 10:32 phone conversation, Bush finally agreed and flew instead to Barksdale Air Force base near Shreveport, Louisiana, landing there at 11:45 a.m. with no military escort until the last five minutes. President Bush's decision to fly more than 750 miles to Louisiana with no security escort is another piece of circumstantial evidence that both Bush and Cheney knew there was no foreign-based threat to the president.

From Bush's body language in the Moore video, we get the impression that the president was well satisfied with events up until he was airborne at 10 a.m. (setting aside the foiled assassination attempt). The months-long planning for the big day of 9/11 homegrown terror had finally arrived.

Although he was not the quarterback, he was the most high-profile member of the team that planned and executed perhaps history's most stunning false-flag operation. President Bush was fully invested in the conspirators' goal to transform America's imperial mission and radically change the world.

But the president's copacetic frame of mind was soon to be overturned when he was informed that Cheney had in mind a change of plan. President Bush's early resumption of his executive powers would be delayed – for who knows how long?

Bush's frustration and attempted push-back at this unanticipated turnabout is a clue that all the planned terror events of 9/11 were to be completed by 10 a.m. Bush had proceeded to Florida with the understanding that he would stretch out his photo-op at Booker Elementary and remain out of the chain of command until then. He understood that the plan was that after 10 a.m. he was to fly back to Washington.

What did Bush make of Cheney's rationale that the threats to Air Force One required a detour or two? The central fact was clear: Cheney was maintaining control of the government. President Bush may well have suspected a sinister motive. Did one of the many rumors of ongoing terror threats mask Cheney's plan to assassinate him?

In any case, at Barksdale, Bush was once again on the losing side of the question of where he should go next. He spent much of his time at Barksdale arguing with Cheney. When a frustrated President Bush insisted to his aide Karl Rove that he wanted to return to Washington, the latter replied, "Our people are saying it's unstable still." Bush once again gave in and when he left Barksdale around 1:30 p.m. it was not for D.C. but for Offutt Air Base in Nebraska. He was told that he could get to the U.S. Strategic Command Center there quicker than he could fly to Washington.

Finally, Bush was allowed to or insisted on his return to Washington. Bush left Offutt at 4:30 p.m. and reached Andrews Air Force Base at 6:34 p.m. From there he helicoptered to the White House which he reached at 7 p.m. At 8:30 p.m. he gave a five-minute nationally televised speech threatening revenge on the terrorists and those who harbored them.

President George W. Bush was back in control.

***

Epilogue

Did Cheney actually plan to assassinate President Bush? It's hardly likely we'll ever get to the bottom of this question since it didn't happen. But is it so far-fetched? Would it not have been similarly far-fetched to consider that President Kennedy would be assassinated in broad daylight in Dallas 38 years earlier had it not actually happened?

How do we explain the early morning assassination attempt of President Bush at Longboat Key? As we have seen, evidence points to the involvement of elements of U.S. security and intelligence agencies, including the CIA and the FBI, well within the control of the vice president. How do we explain President Bush's negligent behavior from 8:46 a.m. to 10 a.m.? How do we explain Vice President Cheney's unwonted change of plan, refusing to allow President Bush his expected early return to the White House? Surely the sinister theory deserves consideration.

How ambitious was Dick Cheney? Cheney was a larger-than-life force of nature without whom there would have been no 9/11, and perhaps no Bush presidency. Are there many who doubt that had the early assassination attempt on President Bush's life succeeded, Cheney would have welcomed the opportunity to move into the White House? The only question was whether he actively, treacherously, had such plans.

What sort of a world are we living in? If the underlying assumptions of this paper are correct, we're manifestly living in the world of the big lie. Perhaps that's the natural order of things in nation states where scores and hundreds of millions of people have to find ways of living in comity. To do so, we perforce delegate authority, all too often to those of ruthless ambition.

Where do justice and the rule of law come in? As Dickens's Artful Dodger in *Oliver Twist* found, "This ain't the shop for justice."[145]

Notes

[1]David Ray Griffin's first book on 9/11 *The New Pearl Harbor: Disturbing Questions About the Bush Administration and 9/11* appeared in 2004. His second, *The 9/11 Commission Report: Omissions and Distortions*, was published a year later. My first article summarizing some of the critical issues exposed by Griffin's books was originally intended as the first of two, but as noted above, my views changed. Aside from its historical value, my article contains pertinent sections indirectly supporting the NPT as well as looking into President George W. Bush's eyebrow-raising actions on 9/11 and after, and other 9/11 anomalies.

[2]See for example: "Debunked: Pilots for 9/11 truth WTC speeds"

[3]See Hani Hanjour: 9/11 Pilot Extraordinaire, "[for pilot John Lear's affidavit citing circumstantial evidence that no pilots, experienced or not, could have struck the Twin Towers with a passenger plane.

[4]One of the "expert" witnesses who pointed to Bin Laden's responsibility for the 9/11 attacks was none other than Paul Bremer, appointed as Czar of Iraq (2003-2004). One can posit a through-line between Bremer's comments on 9.11.01 and his disastrous tenure in Iraq where he played a key role in insuring civil war. Bremer's appointment reveals that the point of the U.S. invasion was to destroy Iraq's civil life..

[5]See e.g. The Pentagon Flyover - How They Pulled It Off and Matt Sullivan 2013 "The Pentagon Flyover Theory"

[6] See Gerard Holmgren's debunking article, The Naudet video of the Nth Tower strike was staged with full foreknowledge of what was about to happen.) I suppose that readers who find Holmgren's argument plausible will conclude that if the video of the first strike was staged, the same is likely to be true of the second.

[7]This episode is cited in my No Planes on 911 - the two minute video.

[8] Robert Fisk: Even I question the 'truth' about 9/11 (August 2007)

Here's the first paragraph of Fisk's article:

"Each time I lecture abroad on the Middle East, there is always someone in the audience – just one – whom I call the "raver."

Apologies here to all the men and women who come to my talks with bright and pertinent questions – often quite humbling ones for me as a journalist – and which show that they understand the Middle East tragedy a lot better than the journalists who report it. But the 'raver'is real. He has turned up in corporeal form in Stockholm and in Oxford, in Sao Paulo and in Yerevan, in Cairo, in Los Angeles and, in female form, in Barcelona. No matter the country, there will always be a 'raver.'" For an open letter responding to Fisk's article see H.Fenton: Open Letter to Robert Fisk re 911 Truth or Conspiracy, published on 911blogger.com.

[9] Alexander Cockburn still believes in the Warren Commission and its 'magic bullet.' He makes his political motives quite clear: "These days a dwindling number of leftists learn their political economy from Marx..." a fact he deplores.

If they had they would have been able to resist the "diffuse, peripatic (sic) conspiracist view of the world that tends to locate ruling class devilry not in the crises of capital accumulation, or the falling rate of profit, or inter-imperial competition, but in locale (the Bohemian Grove, Bilderberg, Ditchley, Davos) or supposedly "rogue" agencies, with the CIA still at the head of the list." https://www.counterpunch.org/2018/04/20/syria-and-neo-mccarthyism/

As he makes very clear, his refusal to examine the evidence is rooted in his a priori view that everything can and ought to be explained in terms of Marxist theories of vast anonymous forces such as capitalist accumulation and the falling rate of profit. Conspiracies, he thinks, are more to the taste of "the libertarian and populist right" which "mistrusts government to a far greater degree than the left..." Obviously, after mastering Volume Three of Capital, one has no need of empirical evidence, even if Marx never did get around to writing his book on the State.

Cockburn -- as well as Chomsky -- know in advance that all US presidents are all equally servants of ruling class interests and that therefore it wouldn't make any political sense to assassinate them, ergo an assassination is merely a FAIT DIVERS [CURRENT EVENT], devoid of political significance, ergo the bullets all came from the sixth floor of the Book Depository.

Cockburn also asks: What do we make of Osama taking credit for the attacks? That he's still on the CIA payroll?" The fact is that Osama explicitly denied having anything to do with the attacks and indeed condemned them. http://www.robert-fisk.com/usama_interview_ummat.htm

After denying and condemning it publicly, he then is supposed to have made a private video, claiming credit for what he publicly denied, and condemned, and somehow allowed it to fall into the hands of the Americans.

[10] He might begin by going back to his interview with Bin Laden, where he encountered a man seemingly cut off from what was happening in the world (he devoured a two-week old newspaper that Fisk was carrying in his backpack). Is it possible to reconcile that with the idea that such a man could have been the "mastermind" of this complicated and ramified plot. (He might also care to reread the interview with Bin Laden referred to above.

[11] Cockburn goes him one better: After flinging the word "idiocy" against David Ray Griffin's claim that..."In light of standard procedures for dealing with hijacked airplanes not one of these planes should have reached its target, let alone all three of them," Cockburn goes on to claim: "A central characteristic of the conspiracists is that they have a devout, albeit preposterous belief in American efficiency. Many of them start with the racist premise--frequently voiced in as many words in their writings -- that "Arabs in caves" weren't capable of the mission." It is hard to recognize in such gratuitous accusations of "idiocy" and "racism" any sign of genuine conviction or dedication to finding the truth. Rather such name calling appears to be a desperate attempt to discredit the motives of those who differ.

[12] The bad news is that by mid-May 2019, the accounts for one of the most reliable sources for 9/11 truth, 911research.wtc7.net has been suspended. Any relevant information would be most welcome.

[13] The New Pearl Harbor: Disturbing Questions About the Bush Administration and 9/11 by David Ray Griffin Published by Interlink, March 1, 2004.

[14] Quoted in Griffin, *The New Pearl Harbor*, p. 177.

[15] Videos still available of the collapse of WTC 7 (May 2019) see e.g. https://www.youtube.com/watch?v=7ZiMG84hws0
Building weakened by WTC attack collapses 1.24

https://www.youtube.com/watch?v=xrzeN-wvHD4
WTC 7 Collapse Full - Do you hear explosives? .23

https://www.youtube.com/watch?v=g3Tg9bM-PGw
The explosions which were part of the controlled demolition are visible and are slowed down for visibility on repeat showing. 1:11 / 1:14

This video includes Larry Silverstein apparently agreeing to the controlled demolition destruction of WTC 7: He says: "… and we made that decision to pull it and we watched the building collapse." https://www.youtube.com/watch?v=tBcKVAdJ6U0
9/11 - 7 World Trade Center (WTC 7 Free Fall Collapse)
With pro and con sound bite testimony from experts and others. 1:33 / 7:52 https://www.youtube.com/watch?v=LD06SAf0p9A
This video is 10 seconds long including bystander reaction
Jim Hoffman's 2003 slide show presentation can be found at
http://911research.wtc7.net/talks/b7/index.html

[16] http://911research.wtc7.net/talks/towers/introduction.html

[17] Eric Hufschmid, *Painful Questions: An Analysis of the September 11th Attack* (California, End Point Software, 2002), p. 82. See http://www.hugequestions.com/Eric/PainfulQuestionsBook.html

[18] Larry Silverstein's comment about "pulling" Building 7 was made in a September 2002 PBS documentary, "America Rebuilds." ." See http://www.rense.com/Datapages/WTC7.htm for more information and discussion of this and related WTC 7 issues.

[19] See Griffin, *The New Pearl Harbor*, p. 185.

[20] Eric Hufschmid is particularly good on this aspect of the 9/11 attacks. His description of how the homing device may have operated to crash two aircraft into the Twin Towers provides an explanation of

why the plane that hit the South Tower, took a circular route and hit the building from the south instead of flying directly into the Tower from its northerly origin. See *Painful Questions*, pp. 90-92.

[21] http://911research.wtc7.net/wtc/background/owners.html According to Don Paul Larry Silverstein already controlled more than 8 million square feet of New York City Real Estate. He also owned Runway 69, a nightclub in Queens that was alleged to be laundering money made through sales of Laotian heroin.

[22]Griffin, The *New Pearl Harbor*, pp. 183-84.

[23]Hufschmid's discussion of this theory will be found on *Painful Questions*, pp. 82-84.

[24]Those in the 9/11 Truth movement point out that the use of the word hijacker concedes a part of the U.S. government's official story, one for which no evidence has been presented.

[25]William Thomas, *Stand Down: Why America's Air Defenses Failed on Sept 11*

[26]David Ray Griffin: THE NEW PEARL HARBOR DISTURBING QUESTIONS ABOUT THE BUSH ADMINISTRATION AND 9/11, Massachusetts: Olive Branch Press (2004)
David Ray Griffin: THE 9/11 COMMISSION REPORT: OMISSIONS AND DISTORTIONS, MASSACHUSETTS: Olive Branch Press (2005)

[27]Paul Thompson, *The Terror Timeline*, New York: HarperCollins Publishers Inc. 2004. Griffin began working with the *Timeline* when it was available only on the Internet.

[28]*The New Pearl Harbor* is now available free on the Internet at Houston Indymedia.

[29]Some of these times are in dispute. The 9/11 Commission often gives later times apparently in order to paper over the lack of a military response to the attacks.

As Griffin indicates, despite news reports at the time giving 8:15 for the loss of AA 11's transponder signal, the 9/11 Commission, "entirely on the basis of interviews puts the time at 8:21," and Northeast Air Defense Sector (NEADS) put the time even later, sometime after 8:30. (O&D, p. 321, note 3).

Some 9/11 skeptics present plausible arguments suggesting that no commercial passenger jets struck the Twin Towers or the Pentagon. It's not clear how this avenue of research would affect Griffin's and others' investigations of the air defense stand-down. It would seem that much of the information would remain relevant if only to show the inadequacy of the official story. For more information, see Gerard Holmgren, "Manufactured Terrorism: The Truth About Sept 11." http://911closeup.com/

[30]Michael C. Ruppert, *Crossing the Rubicon: The Decline of the American Empire At the End of the Age of Oil* , New Society Publishers: Gabriola Island, BC, (2004), pp. 310-312.
Guillaume wonders what happened to the tape recordings of controller and pilot conversations that many would assume to be a matter of public record. (p. 313)

[31]*Pentagate*, U.K.: Carnot Publishing Ltd. (2002), p. 90. The language has been slightly modified and colloquialzed by Laura Knight-Jadczyk, "Comments on the Pentagon Strike, (undated, February 2005?), *http://www.cassiopaea.org/cass/boeing.htm* All emphasis is hers.

[32]On "Meet the Press" (9/16/01) "when Tim Russert…expressed surprise that although we knew about the first hijacking by 8:20, "it seems we were not able to scramble fighter jets in time to protect the Pentagon." Cheney did not dispute this statement" and made no

reference to jets being scrambled too late. (NPH, 8 & note 19, p. 208). In addition, Major Mike Snyder, NORAD spokesman, said that no fighters were scrambled until after the Pentagon was hit. *Boston Globe* 9/15/01.

[33]General Meyers's testimony was publicly recognized as problematic by Senators Carl Levin and Bill Nelson who wanted to know why no jets were scrambled "until after the Pentagon was hit." Senator Nelson suggested that, if necessary, the "exact timelines" should be reviewed in executive session. /http://emperors-clothes.com/9-11backups/mycon.htm

[34]'Guilty for 9-11, Part 1: What Happened to the Air Force on September 11th?" by Illarion Bykov and Jared Israel /http://emperors-clothes.com/indict/indict-1.htm

[35]The third version of the official explanation for the apparent air defense stand-down is the 9/11 Commission's attempt to fix the problems with NORAD's 9/18 timeline since military jets should have intercepted the passenger planes even allowing for NORAD's new times. As Griffin points out, this fix came almost two years after 9/11/01. Griffin reasons that if this 2nd version was a result of mistakes or lying and it went uncorrected for that long, why we should have to take the government's word that this third version by the 911 Commission is not a similar product.

[36]Otis AFB is in Massachusetts. It's not clear why jets weren't scrambled from the closer Andrews AFB in New Jersey.

[37]911 Timeline of some key events mentioned in the text. Times are generally those given by David Ray Griffin.
8:12-8:15 radio and transponder contact with AA Flight 11 lost
8:14 UA Flight 175 leaves Boston
 8:20 Bush says farewell to management at Colony Beach and Tennis resort

Fl 11 veers widely off course
8:24 FAA hears hijackers in cockpit of Fl 11 indicate that a hijacking was in progress
8:35 Bush's motorcade leaves hotel

8:37 9/11 Commission reports that FAA notified the military regarding problems with AA Flight 11. Jets scrambled from Otis AFB soon afterwards.
8:38 (Second version of official story) Military informed of problems with AA Fl 11.
8:42 UA 175 radio and transponder went off and it veered off course. NORAD notified at 8:43 (2nd version of the official story)
8:46 First terror strike hits WTC North Tower
8:55 All clear announcement at WTC South Tower
Bush arrives at Booker elementary right around this time
9:03 Terror strike on WTC South Tower
9:38 Pentagon strike

[38]PAVE is a program name for electronic systems. PAWS stands for Phased Array Warning System. /http://www.pavepaws.org.

[39]*Pentagate, op. cit*, p. 115. Once again, I use Laura Knight-Jadczyk's somewhat more colloquial version, "Comments on the Pentagon Strike" *op.cit*. Her emphasis.

[40]Griffin explains that the 9/11 Commission, sometimes known as the Kean Commission, should more properly be referred to as the Kean-Zelikow Commission because of the influence of its executive director, Philip Zelikow, and his efforts to shield the military and the Bush administration from charges of complicity in the attacks. (O&D, 6-14)

[41]Quoted in Allan Wood, Paul Thompson, "An Interesting Day: President Bush's Movements and Actions on 9/11"
http://cooperativeresearch.org/essay.jsp?article=essayaninterestin gday

[42] *Ibid*. Bush said farewell to the management at the Colony Beach and Tennis Resort at 8:20 a.m.

[43] http://www.cooperativeresearch.org/timeline.jsp?timeline=complete _911_timeline&timeperiod=1:00am%20Sept%2011%202001   (All timeline references are to this url unless otherwise indicated.)

[44] Thompson and Allen record seven different accounts of how Bush learned about the first crash: in his limousine, from Loewer, from Card, from Rove, from Gottesman, from Rice, from television. "An Interesting Day," *op. cit.*

[45] FAA = the Federal Aviation Administration,
NORAD= North American Aerospace Defense Command; HQ: Colorado Springs; divided into various sectors, only one of which was involved on 9/11; NEADS, The Northeast Air Defense Sector NMCC =National Military Command Center located in the Joint Staff area of the Pentagon, Washington, D.C. According to French critic, Thierry Meyssan, the NMCC "centralizes all information concerning plane hijackings and directs military operations." *Pentagate, op.cit.* p. 117.

[46] Jared Israel and Francisco Gil-White "Bush Gets Tangled in his 9-11 Lies, Part I: A Strange White House Press Conference," Posted 25 September 2002, Updated 27 September 2002. ///http://emperors-clothes.com/indict/calif1.htm

[47] Quoted in "The President as Incompetent Liar: Bush's Claim that he Saw TV Footage of 1st Plane Hitting WTC." Comments by Jared Israel. [Posted 12 September 2002]

[48]"President Meets with Displaced Workers in Town Hall Meeting, Remarks by the President in Town Hall Meeting Orange County Convention Center, Orlando, Florida." There is a slight discrepancy between Ari Fleischer's account and the one Bush gave at his December and January 2002 Town Hall meetings. Fleischer said Bush learned of the first strike when he first arrived at the school and was informed by members of his staff whereas Bush said that he saw what happened in real time on TV when he was already in the school. Nevertheless, both versions have in common that no one in the presidential party knew until Bush was already in the classroom at 9:03 that the U.S. had suffered a terror attack. Both versions present an alibi for going forward with the photo op.

In his January Town Hall meeting in California, Bush made similar comments about when he learned of the first plane strike and that at first, he thought it was an accident. "President Holds Town Hall Forum on Economy in California, Remarks by the President in Town Hall Meeting with Citizens of Ontario, Ontario Convention Center, Ontario, California," California Town Meeting. January 5, 2002. /http://www.whitehouse.gov/news/releases/2002/01/20020105-3.html

[49]Critics note that school principal Rigell's testimony contradicts Bush's account at these town hall meetings. Thompson calls Bush's claim that he saw the first strike on live TV "preposterous." Years later, the *Wall St Journal* reported that a Bush spokesman later called Bush's memory of the events, "just a mistaken recollection." (3/22/04) "An Interesting Day," *op. cit.*

[50]See NPH, pp. 62-63.

[51]Michael C. Ruppert, *Crossing the Rubicon: op.cit.*, p. 434.

[52]*Against All Enemies: Inside America's War on Terror* (March 2004)

[53]In accordance with standard procedure, several teleconferences or phone bridges were set up that day to link various agencies. One of these was initiated by the NMCC.

[54]The 9:29 a.m. talk was previously intended to focus on education issues.

[55]*Fighting Back: The War on Terrorism from Inside the Bush White House* (October 2002)

[56]See Paul O'Neil's book *The Price of Loyalty*. The former Secretary of the Treasury wrote that, c, at the very first Cabinet meeting of the new Bush government in January 2001, high on the agenda was the plan to attack Iraq. For evidence that Bush predicted the attack Iraq while he was still a candidate, see the interview on *Democracy Now* where candidate Bush assured a Muslim leader in Michigan on the campaign trail in the spring of 2000 that Saddam Hussein would be removed. In addition, the neocon plan to invade Iraq was a matter of public record since the aftermath of the first Gulf War in 1991. Bush's campaign remarks are also interesting because they are evidence that he was aware that the Florida election (and doubtless others) would be rigged in his favor.

[57]I later learned that as President Eisenhower approved the plan to overthrow Castro. He must have been enraged when JFK refused to follow his lead.

[58]Videos still available of the collapse of WTC 7 (May 2019) see e.g.
https://www.youtube.com/watch?v=7ZiMG84hws0
Building weakened by WTC attack collapses 1.24
https://www.youtube.com/watch?v=xrzeN-wvHD4
WTC 7 Collapse Full - Do you hear explosives? .23
https://www.youtube.com/watch?v=g3Tg9bM-PGw

[59]A figure of speech in which the natural or rational order of its terms is reversed, as in *bred and born* instead of *born and bred*.

[60]It appeared for a time that the problem might simply be that the parties who turned up this broadcast footage had confused standard and daylight-saving time; or perhaps that they had identified some other building as WTC 7—but the BBC doesn't assert either of those defenses. Rather, it says its magically prescient reporting was a "cock up," a mistake on a chaotic day. CNN likewise forgoes any such defense.

[61]The same FEMA that did "a heck of a job" with Hurricane Katrina. What expertise FEMA has (if any) in the design, engineering or construction of skyscrapers is a mystery.

One might have expected the 9/11 Commission to take testimony from architects and engineers or appoint neutral experts to investigate and report. Moreover, if flimsy construction were a cause but for which the towers would not have collapsed, there would surely have been litigation, which has never materialized.

[62]Ganser also describes (p. 29) secret protocols under which Italy would be kept in alignment with the West "by any means" necessary, even if its electorate voted otherwise, and under which West Germany, as a condition of its admission to NATO in 1955, agreed to refrain from active legal pursuit of known right-wing extremists.

[63]Relations between the CIA and the mob remained cordial, as with their joint attempts to assassinate Fidel Castro in the 1960s, a matter brought to light in the Church Committee hearings of the 1970s. See, e.g., Peter Dale Scott, *The War Conspiracy*, p. 35 (1972); and Scott's book *Deep Politics and the Death of JFK* (University of California Press, 1993). Scott is particularly interested in the CIA's complicity in drug trafficking.

[64]The *Times* article reports that "Mr. Bush was accompanied at the meeting by Condoleezza Rice, who was then the national security adviser; Dan Fried, a senior aide to Ms. Rice; and Andrew H. Card Jr., the White House chief of staff. Along with Mr. Manning, Mr. Blair

was joined by two other senior aides: Jonathan Powell, his chief of staff, and Matthew Rycroft, a foreign policy aide and the author of the Downing Street memo." The "Downing Street memo" is the famous document of July 23, 2002, that says ". . . the intelligence and facts were being fixed around the policy [of war on Iraq]"—rather than the war policy being a response to intelligence or facts.

[65]For another aspect of the culture, having to do with CIA infiltration of the news media, search on "Operation Mockingbird." The leading article is Carl Bernstein, "The CIA and the Media," *Rolling Stone*, Oct. 20, 1977.

As to a similar problem, also relevant in this case, see Alison Weir, "U.S. Media Coverage of Israel and Palestine: Choosing Sides," in Peter Phillips, ed., *Censored 2005: The Top 25 Censored Stories* (2004). Cf. Alfred M. Lilienthal, in *The Washington Report on Middle East Affairs*, June, 1989 (available online) as to the near demise of the New York *Times* in the late 1940s when Arthur Hays Sulzberger rebuked the Zionists for their "coercive methods" and "attempts at character assassination," a mistake he and his successors have avoided making again. The *Washington Report* is published by the American Educational Trust, founded by retired Foreign Service officers. Two former chairmen of the Senate Foreign Relations Committee have sat on its board, J. William Fulbright (D. Ark.) and Charles H. Percy (R. Ill).

[66]In early April 2007 it came out that Walter Murphy, McCormick Professor of Jurisprudence Emeritus at Princeton, had found himself on the national terrorist watchlist (i.e., the no-fly list). Murphy's sin was giving a televised lecture last fall on Bush's transgressions against the Constitution. The no-fly list was used earlier to punish Doug Thompson, the editor of *CapitolHillBlue.com*. Thompson had published a series of articles on George W. Bush's psychological problems. Thompson's sources included anonymous White House staffers—and Justin Frank, M.D., a psychiatrist at the George Washington University School of Medicine. Frank considers Bush a classic "dry drunk," unable to deal with reality or responsibility, except that he has serious doubts about the "dry" part.

[67]Full disclosure: I've been a lifelong Democrat and a critic of the Bush administration from the moment they were selected by the Supreme Court in 2000.

[68]Gerard Holmgren, "Manufactured Terrorism – The Truth About Sept 11," (2004, revised 2006).
http://www.supremelaw.org/authors/holmgren/911.Closeup.2.html

[69]Morgan Reynolds, "We Have Some Holes in the Plane Stories," (March 2006).
http://nomoregames.net/index.php?page=911&subpage1=we_have_holes

[70]According to Peter Dale Scott, the alleged hijackers were identified as early as 10 a.m. "JFK and 911," (December 2006).
http://www.globalresearch.ca/index.php?context=viewArticle&code=SCO20061220&articleId=4207

[71]Quoted in David Ray Griffin, *The New Pearl Harbor: Disturbing Questions About the Bush Administration and 9/11 (2004)*, [NPH] p. 177.

72See Jim Hoffman's website:
http://911research.wtc7.net/wtc/analysis/compare/fires.html#ref1
The website includes details and photos of other large fires which did not result in the collapse of steel framed buildings such as: the First Interstate Fire (1988), the One New York Plaza Fire (1970), the Caracas Tower Fire (2004) and the even more severe Windsor Building Fire (2005). Hoffman's site also contains essays critically analyzing some of the reports, which have been produced to support the official version in *Popular Mechanics, Scientific American* and the NIST report on the collapse of the Twin Towers.

73Quoted in NPH, pp. 12-13.

74Eric Hufschmid, *Painful Questions: An Analysis of the September 11th Attack* (2002).

75Gerard Holmgren, "Manufactured Terrorism: The Truth About Sept 11."

76The first official explanation, quickly discarded, was that there were no military jet interceptions until after the Pentagon was hit at 9:37. This explanation, apparently the truth, is consistent with the No Planes Theory.

77NPH, p. 6. Vice President Cheney did much to confuse the issue when he spoke of the requirement for Presidential authorization to shoot down a civilian aircraft. Interceptions without shoot downs, on the other hand are routine and don't require high-level authorization. Griffin and others emphasize that in extreme emergencies even shoot downs are permitted without top-level authorization.

78See for example YouTube video: "Did Flight 93 Crash in Shanksville?"

79Morgan Reynolds, "Revisiting the WTC Building Collapses, Part I." (July 2005) http://nomoregames.net/index.php?page=911&subpage1=revisiting_the_WTC_collapses

[80]All references to Reynolds are to his article, "We Have Some Holes in the Plane Stories," (March 2006) unless otherwise indicated.
http://nomoregames.net/index.php?page=911&subpage1=we_have_holes

[81]Manufactured Terrorism: The Truth About Sept 11."

[82]See below for the excerpt from Elias Davidsson's *Betrayal of America* regarding the lack of evidence of for hijackers.

[83]Holmgren documents some of his assertions with links to the section of his website on the Pentagon:
http://members.iinet.com.au/~holmgren/pentagon.html, which includes: A phantom plane. June 2002; Hunt the Boeing; The amazing pentalawn; Killtown's Pentagon research; Physical analysis of Pentagon crash. Oct 2002.

[84]See Gerard Holmgren's essay arguing that not one single eyewitness to a large plane at the Pentagon can be trusted. "Did AA 77 Really Hit the Pentagon: (Eyewitness accounts examined,"
http://members.iinet.net.au/~holmgren/witness.html; see also: Gerard Holmgren, "What Witnesses?
http://www.911closeup.com/index.shtml?ID=84

[85]See Gerard Holmgren, "What really happened to American Airlines Flights 11 and 77 on Sept 11, 2001"

http://www.angelfire.com/trek/chucheeshouse/untying/911hoax.html and "Manufactured Terrorism." Both UA 175, plane number N612UA and UA 93, plane number N591UA, were "still registered and valid more than 4 years after [their] alleged destruction." Holmgren, "Manufactured Terrorism.

[86] See Holmgren's documents page at:
http://members.iinet.net.au/~holmgren/nthtower.html

[87] Ivan Amato explains how video can be manipulated in real time – as in the ability of TV technicians to lay down first down lines in real time in a football game.

[88] Gerard Holmgren, "The Videos of the Plane Hitting the South Tower are Faked. The Plane is a Cartoon. (http://members.iinet.com.au/~holmgren/sthtower.html)

[89] More claims that Holmgren makes about video of the second plane include:

*The hole in the South Tower only "appears well after the plane has entirely disappeared without disturbing the building."

*It exceeds the maximum speed of a Boeing 767 at low altitude while banked sharply and flying in the opposite direction to that which it's banking.

*It hip hops across the screen regularly alternating, frame-by-frame, between supersonic speed and hovering motionless.

*It has a strange anomaly in the shape of the belly.

*Different videos of the plane contradict each other as to the flight path of the plane's approach.

[90] See for example, The Incredible 911 Evidence We've All Been Overlooking

[91] Holmgren --Why They Didn't Use Planes

[92] Eric Hufschmid, *Painful Questions*, *op. cit.*, note 6.

[93]Vincent Sammartino, The 911 Passenger List Oddity

[94]NPR gives the total number of passengers and crew killed as 246 (All Things Considered, Nov 17, 2006). Yet, according to standdown.net, "when one adds up the 4 official death manifest lists published on CNN.com, there are only 229 names.
The total seating capacity of the four airliners "of September 11th, 2 Boeing 767s and 2 Boeing 757s" was 762 people." (standdown.net).

[95]See NPH, pp. 27-28. See also for example, "Those Fabricated Cell Phone Calls,"
http://www.serendipity.li/wtc4.htm#cellphone_calls; and, among others, "The Cellphone and Airfone Calls from Flight UA93," http://physics911.net/cellphoneflight93.htm.
See "Bleier 911 The Two Minute Video" (2015) explaining that the cell phone calls were suborned, scripted, and made from the ground.

[96]A meme is a unit of cultural information that is transmitted by repetition and imitation.

[97]See note 4 above.

[98]Scripps Howard News Service (August 2006)
http://www.abqtrib.com/albq/nw_national_government/article/0,2564 ,ALBQ_19861_4894025,00.html

Yet these numbers need to be seen in context. Only 16% believe that explosives were used to bring down the WTC Towers and only 12% believe that a passenger jet didn't crash into the Pentagon. And 38% believe that "the federal government is withholding proof of the existence of intelligent life from other planets."

[99]See David Ray Griffin's discussion, NPH, pp. xi-xii.

[100]Naomi Klein, "Baghdad Year Zero," *Harper's Magazine*, September 2004.[92] Naomi Klein, "Baghdad Year Zero," *Harper's Magazine*, September 2004.

[101]Lance deHaven-Smith, *Conspiracy Theory in America* (Austin: U of Texas P, 2013) p. 14.

[102]ibid.

[103]Michael Dorman, "Hijackers' lost luggage conveniently solves so many 9/11 mysteries." Newsday, April 17 2006. Republished with acerbic commentary at http://www.unknownnews.org/0604180417lostluggage.html .

[104]Jay Kolar, "What We Now Know About the Alleged 9/11 Hijackers." In Paul Zarembka, Ed., *The Hidden History of 9/11* (NY: Seven Stories Press, 2011) pp. 3 - 44.

[105]Charles Kurzman, "Al-Qaeda as Fringe Cult: 12 Years Later, Heretical Text of 9/11 Hijackers Still Withheld by FBI." http://www.juancole.com/2013/09/heretical-hijackers-withheld.html

[106]The New Yorker 10/8/2001, cited at http://www.historycommons.org/context.jsp?item=a0901deliberatetrai l.

[107]On 9/11-anthrax as a single false flag operation, see Graeme MacQueen, *The 2001 Anthrax Deception.* Atlanta, GA: Clarity Press, 2014.

[108]Project for a New American Century (PNAC), "Rebuilding America's Defenses: Strategy, Forces, and Resources for a New Century." September 2000. http://www.informationclearinghouse.info/pdf/RebuildingAmericasD efenses.pdf.

[109]John Deutch and Philip Zelikow, "Catastrophic Terrorism: Tackling the New Danger." *Foreign Affairs,* November-December 1998. http://www.foreignaffairs.com/articles/54602/ashton-b-carter-john-deutch-and-philip-zelikow/catastrophic-terrorism-tackling-the-new-danger.

[110]"Thinking about Political History", Miller Center Report, Winter 1999, pp. 5-7.

[111]Ralph Blumenthal, "Tapes Depict Proposal to Thwart Bomb Used in Trade Center Blast." *New York Times,* October 28th, 1993, p.A1. http://www.nytimes.com/1993/10/28/nyregion/tapes-depict-proposal-to-thwart-bomb-used-in-trade-center-blast.html?pagewanted=all&src=pm.

[112]ibid.

[113]Ralph Schoenman, "Who Bombed the U.S. World Trade Center? – 1993 Growing Evidence Points to Role of FBI Operative," Prevailing Winds, Number 3, 1993.

[114]Peter Lance, *Triple Cross: How bin Laden's Master Spy Penetrated the CIA, the Green Berets, and the FBI.* NY: William Morrow, 2009. Summarized by the author, reported at http://www.washingtonsblog.com/2009/06/triple-cross-or-inside-job.html.

[115]Peter Dale Scott, "How the FBI Protected al-Qaeda's Hijacker Trainer." Global Research, October 8th, 2006.

http://www.globalresearch.ca/how-the-fbi-protected-al-qaeda-s-9-11-hijacking-trainer/3422.

[116]ibid.

[117]Hyman G. Rickover, *How the Battleship Maine Was Destroyed* (Washington: Dept. of the Navy, Naval History Division, 1976).

[118]"Al-Ahram Al-Arabi: A High-Ranking Yemenite Intelligence Official Blames the US for the Cole Bombing." Middle East Media Research Institute, July 17th, 2001. http://www.memri.org/report/en/print479.htm.

[119]Joe Vialls, "Bali Micro Nuke - Lack of Radiation Confuses 'Experts' – 'The bomb flashed and exploded like a micro nuke, but our Geiger counters don't show any radiation'." http://www.angelfire.com/me4/al_fikr/Bali_Nuked.htm.

[120]Sidney Jones, "Who are the terrorists in Indonesia? Conspiracy theories over the Bali bombing are rife in Indonesia." *The Observer*, October 27th, 2002.

[121] "Mossad agent Mike Harari implicated in Bali bombing, 9/11 - check out his false passports!" TruthJihad.com blog, February 18th, 2011. http://truthjihad.blogspot.com/2011/02/mossad-agent-mike-harari-implicated-in.html.

[122]Mathieu Miquel, "March 11, 2004. The Madrid 3/11 Bombings: Was it Really an Attack by 'Islamic Terrorists'?" Global Research, November 28th, 2009. http://www.globalresearch.ca/march-11-2004-the-madrid-3-11-bombings-was-it-really-an-attack-by-islamic-terrorists/16424.

[123]Nafeez Ahmed, *The London Bombings: An Independent Inquiry* (London: Duckworth, 2006).

[124]Nick Kollerstrom, *Terror on the Tube: Behind the Veil of 7/7, an Investigation*. Joshua Tree, CA: Progressive Press, 2011.

[125]Nandita Sengupta, "Pak TV channel says 26/11 hatched by Hindu Zionists." The Times of India, December 2nd, 2008.

http://timesofindia.indiatimes.com/india/Pak-TV-channel-says-26/11-hatched-by-Hindu-Zionists/articleshow/3785654.cms?referral=PM.

[126] Adrian Levy and Cathy Scott-Clark, "CIA bin Laden hunter David Headley plotted Mumbai massacre." The Sunday Times, November 3rd, 2013.
http://www.thesundaytimes.co.uk/sto/news/world_news/Asia/article1335376.ece.

[127] Yanira Farray, "US-Indo-Israeli Axis." Veterans Today, July 26th, 2010.

[128] Webster Tarpley, "Major Hasan Of Fort Hood: A Patsy In A Drill Gone Live?" Infowars, November 15th, 2009.
http://www.infowars.com/major-hasan-of-fort-hood-a-patsy-in-a-drill-gone-live/.

[129] Kurt Haskell, "The Colossal Deceit Known as The Underwear Bomber Case." http://haskellfamily.blogspot.com/2011/09/colossal-deceit-known-as-underwear.html.

[130] Jason Rynan, "Underwear Bomber Abdulmutallab: 'Proud to Kill in the Name of God'." February 16th 2012.
http://abcnews.go.com/Blotter/underwear-bomber-abdulmutallab-sentenced-life-prison/story?id=15681576.

[131] "Gordon Duff: Times Square Bombing Part of CIA False Flag Against Pakistan." Veterans Today, May 13th, 2010.
http://www.veteranstoday.com/2010/05/13/gordon-duff-time-square-bombing-part-of-cia-false-flag-against-pakistan/.

[132] Dave Lindorff, "Craft International Services hired guns at the Boston Marathon: Why Such Secrecy about Private Military Contractor's Men Working the Event?" April 25th, 2013.
http://thiscantbehappening.net/node/1718.

[133]Sheila Casey, "False flag theater: Boston bombing involves clearly staged carnage." Truth and Shadows, May 8th 2013, http://truthandshadows.wordpress.com/2013/05/08/false-flag-theatre-boston-bombing-involves-clearly-staged-carnage/.

[134]Dave Lindorff, "Did the FBI Snuff Out a Boston Marathon Bombing Witness? Dark Questions About a Deadly FBI Interrogation in Orlando." Counterpunch, March 24th, 2014. http://www.counterpunch.org/2014/03/24/dark-questions-about-a-deadly-fbi-interrogation-in-orlando/.

[135]F. William Engdahl, "The Boston Bombings and the CIA Connection. Graham Fuller and Uncle Ruslan Tsarnaev." Global Research, May 17th 2013. http://www.globalresearch.ca/the-boston-bombings-and-the-cia-connection-graham-fuller-and-uncle-ruslan-tsarnaev/5335416.

[136]ibid.

[137]James Corbett, "Who Is Graham Fuller?" The Corbett Report, May 8th 2013. http://www.corbettreport.com/who-is-graham-fuller/.

[138]ibid.

[139]"CIA trained ISIL in Jordan: Report." Press TV, June 23rd 2014. http://www.presstv.com/detail/2014/06/23/368231/cia-trained-isil-in-jordan-report/.

[140]Miami Herald, "Who Is Iraq's Abu Bakr al-Baghdadi?" June 13th 2014. http://http//www.miamiherald.com/2014/06/13/v-print/4176171/who-is-iraqs-abu-bakr-al-baghdadi.html

[141]Kevin Barrett, "Who Is Abu Bakr al-Baghdadi?" Press TV, July 14 2014.

[142]Kevin Barrett, *Questioning the War on Terror*, pp. 21-22. Madison, WI: Khadir Press, 2009.

[143]"All Terrorists are Muslims…Except the 94% that Aren't." Loonwatch, January 20th, 2010.
http://www.loonwatch.com/2010/01/not-all-terrorists-are-muslims/.

[144]Shadia Drury, *Leo Strauss and the American Right*. NY: Palgrave, 1999.

[145]Ron Suskind, "Faith, Certainty, and the Presidency of George W. Bush." The New York Times Magazine, October 17th, 2004.
http://www.nytimes.com/2004/10/17/magazine/17BUSH.html?_r=3&ex=1255665600&en=890a96189e162076&ei=5090&partner=rssuserland&.145

[146]David Ray Griffin, Osama *Bin Laden: Dead or Alive* (2009), Chapter 1, pp.1-17.

[147]Morgan Reynolds, "We Have Some Holes in the Plane Stories," (March 2006)

[148]See the following links to nine presentations by Jim Hoffman, five on the World Trade Center in NYC and three on the Pentagon attack.
http://911research.wtc7.net/talks/index.html

[149]For a more detailed one page explanation why the physics are such that the fires in the Twin Towers on 9/11 could not have caused the collapses see Jim Hoffman's, "The Twin Towers' Fires and Their Possible Effects."

[150]John Lear's 9/11 Affadavit of January 28, 2008

[151]Morgan Reynolds, "Revisiting the WTC Building Collapses, Part I "

[152]Ronald Bleier, "Holmgren and Reynolds on No Planes on 911-Exposing the Illusion, "(2006)

[153]*Ibid.*

[154]*Ibid.*

[155]*Ibid.*

[156]The one-off popular culture phenomenon of Oliver Stone's remarkable movie, *JFK* (1992) exposing much of the falsehood of the official story had a remarkable, unprecedented and long lasting effect on public opinion. Wide scale rejection of the conclusions of the Warren Commission is evident even today. ; But the lesson seems to be if there is no official follow up in these cases, and no focused media coverage to stir public protest, there will be no substantive political consequences.

[157]Morgan Reynolds, "We Have Some Holes in the Plane Stories," (March 2006)

[158]See Daniel Hopsicker *Welcome to Terrorland: Mohammed Atta & the 9-11 Cover Up in Florida* (2004) for a detailed account of the lifestyle of Mohammed Atta's and some of the other "hijackers'" in the run up to 9/11 in Florida.

[159]Reynolds felt that the court's dismissal was highly likely if not certain since his case had the potential to expose the 9/11 conspiracy in a formal and high-profile setting. Had his lawsuit gone forward he world have had the opportunity to seek answers from government officials who would be subject to charges of perjury. Reynolds writes that "when push comes to shove" there is no realistic opportunity to get justice because "the powerful will be served."
And since the government would not be able to withstand discovery, it was not surprising that in June 2008 Judge George B. Daniels dismissed his and two other 9/11 lawsuits with prejudice.

[160]http://911scholars.ning.com/profiles/blogs/cell-phone-calls-from-hijacked Cell phone calls from hijacked 911 Airliners were impossible.

[161]Author Elias Davidsson, *Hijacking America's Mind on 9/11: Counterfeiting Evidence* (2013) and documentarian Massimo Mazzucco, September 11 – The New Pearl Harbor.

[162]Allan Wood, Paul Thompson, "An Interesting Day: President Bush's Movements and Actions on 9/11." All the references in this essay to President Bush's movements on 9/11 come from this article for the History Commons website, now available on Google cache, and perhaps elsewhere on the internet.

[163]Quoted in the inestimable R. H. Blyth, *Zen in English Literature and Oriental Classics* (1942).

www.ingramcontent.com/pod-product-compliance
Lightning Source LLC
Chambersburg PA
CBHW061405280526
45784CB00001B/379